The British Isles and N. France

A glossary of places mentioned in the text

○ **Scotland**
1. Scone
2. Bannockburn
3. Falkirk
4. Dunbar
5. Roxburgh

○ **England**
1. Berwick-upon-Tweed
2. Norham
3. Cheviot Hills
4. Carlisle
5. York
6. Conisborough
7. Lincoln
8. Chester
9. Shrewsbury
10. Peterborough
11. Northampton
12. Bury St Edmunds
13. Framlingham
14. Gloucester
15. Burford
16. Oxford
17. St Albans
18. Windsor
19. London
20. Brentwood
21. Wells
22. Salisbury
23. Winchester
24. New Forest
25. Canterbury
26. Dover
27. Sandwich
28. Channel Islands

○ **Wales**
1. Anglesey
2. Beaumaris
3. Caernarvon
4. Conway
5. Snowdon
6. Rhuddlan
7. Harlech
8. Aberystwyth
9. Cardigan
10. Pembroke
11. Caerphilly

○ **Ireland**
1. Clonard
2. Clontarf
3. Dublin
4. Limerick
5. Wexford
6. Waterford

Orkneys

SCOTLAND

IRELAND

WALES

ENGLAND

NORTH SEA

STRAITS OF DOVER

FRANCE

First published 1971
Fourth reprint 1978
Macdonald Educational Ltd
Holywell House, Worship Street
London EC2A 2EN

© Macdonald Educational
Limited 1971
Made and printed by
Hazell Watson & Viney Ltd
Aylesbury
Bucks

Cover designed by Robert Jackson
Edited by Bridget Hadaway and
Sue Jacquemier

ISBN 0 356 03751 7

We wish to thank the following individuals and organisations for their assistance and for making available material in their collections:

Achievements Ltd *page 14*

Aerofilms Ltd *page 17*

American Heritage *pages 9, 81*

Bibliothèque de l'Arsenal, Paris *pages 11, 54*

Bibliothèque Nationale, Paris *pages 9, 81*

Bodleian Library Filmstrips *pages 5, 6, 7, 9, 13, 14, 18, 28, 29, 34, 38, 42, 43, 51, 57, 58, 64, 68, 69, 72*

Boyce, Peter *page 42*

Burgerbibliothek, Berne *page 36*

Cash, Allan J. *page 62*

Chabot *page 49*

Christ Church Cathedral, Dublin *page 45*

City of Manchester Art Galleries *page 47*

Clarendon Press, Oxford *page 12*

Crown Copyright *cover, pages 1, 25, 32, 38, 61, 74, 75, 77, 81, 82, 83*

The Dean and Chapter of Westminster Abbey *pages 59, 63, 71, 72*

Doyle *pages 61, 81*

Evans, Barry *page 65*

Gerson, Mark *pages 13, 18, 24, 61, 81*

Giraudon *page 78*

Gordon Foster, Catherine *pages 8, 19, 36*

The Green Studio, Dublin *page 43*

Guildhall Museum *page 55*

Haggerty, Vana *pages 16, 17*

H.M. Queen Elizabeth II: *the illustration on page 67 is reproduced by gracious permission of Her Majesty the Queen*

Hulton Picture Library *pages 1, 8, 20, 26, 30, 37, 44, 56, 60, 68, 82*

Lincoln's Inn Library *page 57*

Longman *pages 13, 50*

Mansell Collection *pages 1, 5, 9, 14, 15, 19, 30, 37, 48, 54, 84*

Mary Evans Picture Library *page 20*

The Master and Fellows of Corpus Christi College, Cambridge *pages 18, 29, 34, 53, 80*

National Library of Wales *page 80*

National Monuments Record *pages 53, 72, 73*

National Portrait Gallery of Scotland *page 25*

National Library of Scotland: by courtesy of the Duke of Roxburghe *page 24*

Neville, Ralph, *page 47*

Ogilvy, Sir David, Bart. *pages 1, 26*

Pictor Ltd *page 50*

Pierpont Morgan Library *page 39*

Pitkin Pictorial Ltd *page 23*

The President and Fellows of Corpus Christi College, Oxford *pages 6, 7, 13, 68*

Public Record Office *pages 13, 19, 48, 55, 64*

The Queen's College Oxford *page 29*

Ridley, Christopher *page 79*

Royal Exchange: by courtesy of the Gresham Committee *page 51*

Scala *pages 11, 48, 59*

Shackwell, Rodney *page 7*

Simon Field Ltd *page 44*

Snark International *pages 32, 49, 58*

Stothard *cover, page 18*

Tabard Publications Ltd *page 80*

Temple Church *page 35*

The Treasurer and Masters of the Bench of the Inner Temple *page 33*

The Trustees of the British Museum *cover, pages 2, 4, 15, 22, 25, 27, 31, 37, 46, 51, 52, 53, 55, 60, 63, 66, 67, 68, 70, 71*

Universitatsbibliothek, Heidelberg *page 41*

Victoria & Albert Museum *pages 1, 9*

The Walters Art Gallery *page 40*

Macdonald
Educational

R J Unstead

Kings Barons & Serfs

A Pictorial History 1086-1300

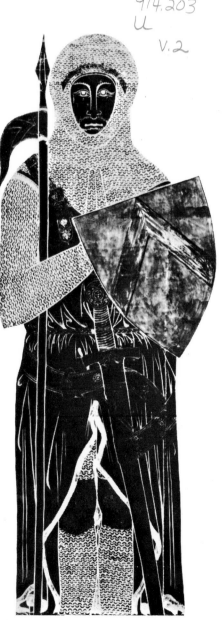

Volume Two

Kings, Barons and Serfs—these were the three classes of society during the period of history that runs from William Rufus's reign to the death of Edward I. At the head of society stood the king, elevated above all men by his God-given authority to rule and by his ownership of all the land in the realm. His barons grouped themselves around him, bound by oath to serve, to obey and to follow him to war. Beneath them lay the serfs, the mass of the people with few rights and no-one to speak for them except the village reeve.

At the beginning of this period, the barons formed a foreign aristocracy, ruling a defeated people by force of arms and possession of the kingdom's strongholds. A depressed peasantry could not threaten them and, since no middle class existed to curb their violence, they were free to quarrel among themselves or to take sides in civil war.

At times, the crown was a prize to be fought for and, in eight reigns covered by this book, every king, except Edward I, had to face armed rebellion and treachery by the barons who were pledged to serve him.

R J Unstead
Kings Barons & Serfs

Contents

Here, on the left, we see the spirit of the age, the obsession of the ruling class. The king and his barons ride against a town and, while they engage its defenders, a common soldier hacks away at the base of the wall. This passion for war carries men to the Crusades, inspires the tournaments and makes up the sides in the civil wars. In this book, we see Englishmen fighting in Ireland, Wales, Scotland and France, in their own country and the Holy Land.

But, we also see a new class emerging silently from the mass of serfs whose labour pays for all the wars. Craftsmen form guilds and run the towns; men buy wool and sell cloth; they build cathedrals and write manuscripts. So far, they have no voice in Parliament and Magna Carta was never meant to refer to them, but, as a class, they are the men who get things done.

A Violent Man- William Rufus

William the Conqueror died in 1087, in Normandy, the duchy in which he was born and in which he spent more time than in England. He could leave his kingdom in capable hands but, in Normandy, he was plagued by unruly barons, by his rebellious sons and by the King of France who tried constantly to weaken his powerful neighbour.

Annoyed by the French, William crossed their frontier and sacked the town of Mantes where his horse stumbled and threw him. He died slowly and in agony from his injuries, leaving behind three sons. They were Robert Curthose, the eldest, William called Rufus, from his reddish colouring, and Henry.

Robert, who had fought his father and wounded him in battle, nevertheless received the duchy of Normandy; Henry was given no land but £5,000 in gold, and to William Rufus went the kingdom of England. This violent man, as cruel and unprincipled as the worst of his barons, tore his father's ring from the dying man's hand and hurried to England to claim the throne.

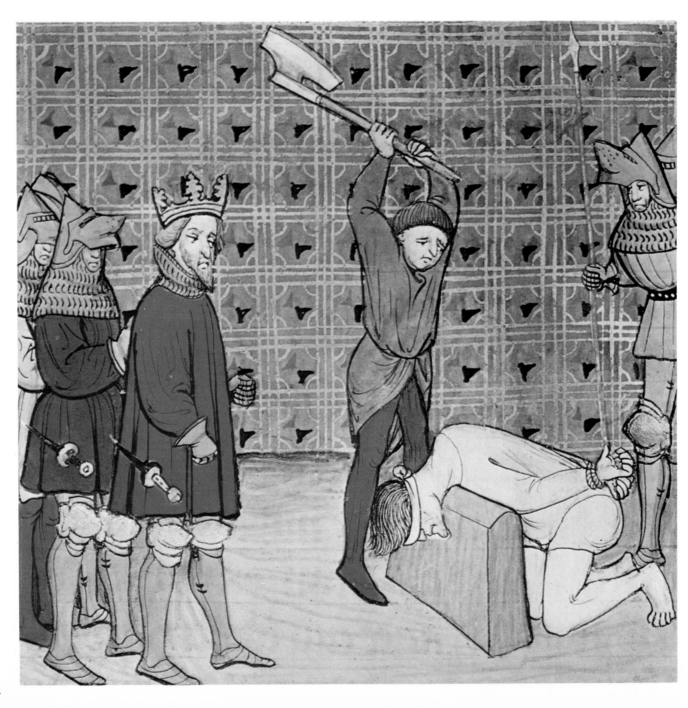

Seal of William Rufus, who is in Norman mail, with spear and shield.

Huntsmen spearing a deer (above) and shooting birds (right). Medieval kings ruthlessly enforced their hunting rights in the forest and no man was allowed to kill game without permission.

William crushes rebellion

William Rufus inherited much of his father's energy and military skill. Almost at once, he had to face a rising of the barons led by his uncle, Bishop Odo; the barons had decided they would prefer the easy-going rule of Robert Curthose to that of his masterful brother. William crushed the rebellion with the help of the English, who readily came to his assistance against their hated oppressors.

He outwitted his brother Robert in Normandy, fought the Welsh, successfully invaded Scotland and thus removed all danger to his own authority. Having made himself even more powerful than his father had been, William set about enriching himself with characteristic Norman greed.

Lanfranc died and, for four years, while no Archbishop of Canterbury was appointed, the King helped himself liberally to the Church's income. He wrung great sums out of the landholders by making every use of his rights. Tenants had to pay certain feudal dues, such as a "relief" when an heir took up his father's land; no-

The king watches an execution (left). As you can see, royal justice was quick and quite heartless.

one disputed the king's right to them, but William demanded far more than the customary dues.

Thus, the barons, the lesser tenants and the Church all hated William. He was undoubtedly cruel, greedy and immoral, and was regarded as a wicked blasphemer. He was, however, so strong and wealthy that none could challenge him. He seemed to be at the height of his career when, at the age of forty, he was suddenly and mysteriously slain.

Death in the forest

With some of his nobles, he set out one day to hunt in the New Forest; the party got split up and, in the evening, a woodman found the King's body with an arrow through the heart. Was it murder or an accident? By some accounts, a nobleman called Sir Walter Tyrrel fired the arrow by accident; William's ambitious brother Henry had every reason to want him dead and there were dark rumours of witchcraft involving the death of a king. At all events, the mystery was never solved. As the chronicler wrote, William "died in the midst of his sins without repentance for his evil deeds". But English people remembered "the good peace he kept in the land".

The Lord and the Villein

When we speak of the "feudal system", we are not using a term that would have been understood by medieval people. The word "feudal" was not used in England until the seventeenth century and "feudalism" much later still. However, the "feudal system" is a convenient way of describing a way of life in which the men gave service (work, gifts, and money) to a landlord in return for land to cultivate, justice and protection. The term also covers the servitude or semi-slavery of the workers and the privileges of the upper classes.

The benefits of the feudal system were that it bound people together at a time when most ordinary folk would have been helpless. A tenant was loyal to his lord, bound to him by an act of homage and an oath of fealty; no man was isolated, he belonged to a community and had his place in society. The disadvantages are more obvious; feudalism gave the ruling class almost complete power over the lives of those who produced food and wealth; it released the nobility from all forms of work except fighting and hunting; it meant privilege for the few, injustice and oppression for the majority.

The king at table (above), food, salt, knife in front of him, wine cup in hand.

The reeve (village overseer) sternly directs the villeins who are reaping wheat on the lord's demesne (estate).

He carries the horn that summons them to work, and the staff with which he is entitled to beat them.

The king out hawking in the forest. On his wrist is a falcon (probably a female peregrine) trained to bring down herons and wild geese.

Payments and duties

A villein was tied to the manor on which he was born. His duties varied in different parts of the country, but they generally depended upon how many strips of land he held in the common fields. One serf, holding 60 strips, might do three days a week of *week-work* for the lord; another serf, holding 20 strips, would do only one day. All duties and rents were recorded in the Manor Roll. Besides work, a man had to pay an annual sum of money, called a *tallage*, and make gifts, usually at Christmas and Easter, of a lamb, a goose or so many eggs. A *boon* was an extra gift and the lord would claim *boon-work* at busy times, like harvest and hay-making.

There were other payments called *reliefs*, such as:
the *heriot*, a villein's best beast, paid to the lord when a villein died.
the *mortuary*, his second best possession, paid to the priest.
the *tithe*, one-tenth of all crops, paid to the church.
the *relief*, paid when a man took over a new holding.
Yet more payments included the hated fee for having corn ground in the lord's mill, the *wood penny* for fallen wood in the forest and the fine to be paid if a son left the manor to enter a monastery, or if a daughter married and left the village. In these cases, the lord was compensated for losing a worker.

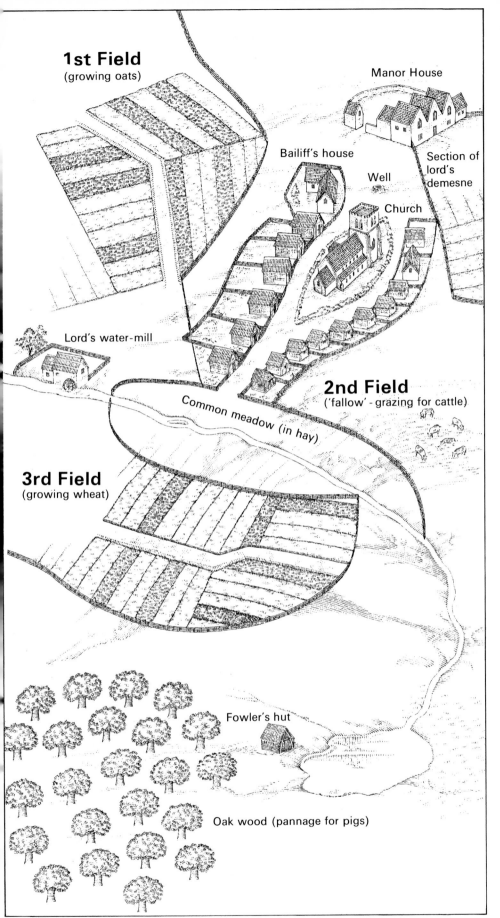

1st Field
(growing oats)

Manor House

Bailiff's house

Well

Section of lord's demesne

Church

Lord's water-mill

Common meadow (in hay)

2nd Field
('fallow' - grazing for cattle)

3rd Field
(growing wheat)

Fowler's hut

Oak wood (pannage for pigs)

Peasant sowing. From the box slung from his neck, he scatters the seed (wheat in autumn, barley and oats in spring) by a rhythmic movement of the arm as he walks. This was a skilled job.

Villagers with authority

The lord's dwelling was a castle or the manor house. If he was a great noble, he owned many manors and came only occasionally to the village. His business manager was the Steward, a busy man who left the everyday running of the village to his assistant, the Bailiff.

This official would order the villagers to do such and such work on the demesne (the lord's land), giving his instructions to the Reeve, a villein chosen by the others to be their spokesman and foreman. He had to see that they carried out their jobs properly and he would beat them if they did not, and bring them before the Manor Court.

Another important villager was the Hayward or Beadle, who acted as village constable for a year, guarding the hay-meadows and collecting fines levied in the Manor Court.

The Priest lived in the village, farmed his land (the "glebe") and stored the tithe corn in the church barn; he was often almost as poor and ignorant as the villagers.

There were several craftsmen whose skills were handed down, father to son—the smith, who made horseshoes and iron tools, the carpenter and the miller. There would also be specialist workers, such as the swineherd, cowherd (or neatherd), shepherd, and the ale-wife, who brewed ale and kept the ale-house.

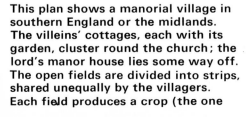

This plan shows a manorial village in southern England or the midlands. The villeins' cottages, each with its garden, cluster round the church; the lord's manor house lies some way off. The open fields are divided into strips, shared unequally by the villagers. Each field produces a crop (the one growing oats would also grow some barley and, probably, peas and beans) and takes its turn to lie "fallow" for a year. This allows the soil to recover strength and provides grazing for cattle. The meadow produces the hay crop for winter feed.

The Crusades Begin

In the seventh and eighth centuries, the Arab followers of the Prophet Mahomet overran Syria, Palestine, Egypt and most of the Middle East. These conquests left the Byzantine Empire, with its glorious capital, Constantinople, as the one Christian stronghold against the infidels. In fact, the Arabs treated the Christians and Jews well; they allowed them to follow their own religions and Christian pilgrims from the West were able to visit the Holy Places in Jerusalem.

Suddenly, the situation changed. In about 1070, the area was overrun by Seljuk Turks from central Asia. These ferocious tribesmen, newly converted to Islam, the religion of Mahomet, captured Jerusalem, occupied Palestine and pressed into Asia Minor to threaten Constantinople itself. The Eastern Emperor, whose best troops had been killed in battle with the Turks, wrote to the Pope, begging him to send a force of the famous Frankish knights. Meanwhile, a trickle of pilgrims returned to the West with stories of their sufferings at the hands of the Turks. The West was ready for a call to arms—Christian knights would save their fellow-Christians in the East.

From the First Crusade, we have to go forward ninety years before we come to an English king playing a leading role in the Crusades. Above is the face of Richard the Lion-heart, as it can be seen in effigy on his tomb.

When he left England on the Third Crusade, the Turks, led by Saladin, had recaptured Jerusalem. The Crusaders' object was to win back the Holy City but it was first necessary to capture the great seaport of Acre.

Richard, already a noted warrior, took Acre by storm but, by his arrogance, he offended Philip Augustus of France and Leopold of Austria. They withdrew their forces, and, although Richard defeated Saladin at Arsouf, his army was not strong enough to capture Jerusalem.

The Pope's call to arms

By the eleventh century, the Pope's authority was immense. Kings and princes obeyed him or, at least, respected his wishes, since he was liable to call upon a neighbouring monarch to punish an offender.

As God's representative on earth, he claimed to be above kings, and when he called on them to take up the Cross, most did so enthusiastically. In the first place, their sins would be forgiven if they could reach Jerusalem and say prayers in the Church of the Holy Sepulchre. If they died in battle on the Crusade, they would go straight to heaven. Furthermore, they loved fighting and many Crusaders hoped to win estates and riches in the East.

In 1096, four well-equipped armies set out on the First Crusade, one commanded by the son of the King of France, one by Godfrey of Bouillon, with knights drawn from northern France and Flanders, one by Raymond of Toulouse and the fourth by the Conqueror's son, Robert of Normandy.

These armies, with a fifth from Italy (Normans led by Prince Bohemond), converged on Constantinople where their quarrels and crude behaviour were highly embarrassing to the Emperor Alexius. However, he sent them into Asia Minor where, after many adventures and disasters, they captured Antioch and pushed on to take the Holy City of Jerusalem in 1099.

Pope Urban II preaching to a vast gathering of Franks at Clermont, 1095 He urged them to take the Cross and free Jerusalem. They cried out "Deus le volt!"—"God wills it!"

The People's Crusade: in 1096, thousands of peasants, led by Peter the Hermit, set out for the Holy Land. Here, you can see them attacked by Hungarians; the survivors were cut to pieces by the Turks in Asia Minor.

How they fought

At the time of the First Crusade, the Frankish knights were the most formidable fighting-men in the world. They relied principally on the power of their massed charge. Clad from head to toe in mail, armed with lance and sword and mounted on their *destriers* (war-horses), they swept lightly-armed forces off the field. In the East, two hundred knights could shatter an army or seize a kingdom.

At first, the Turks were terror-stricken, but they soon learned it was folly to try to meet the Crusaders' charge or to engage them at close quarters.

Instead, they made use of their ponies' superior speed and manoeuvrability to harass the Crusaders on the march, and to dash across their front firing their bows from the saddle at full speed. They would try to divide the marching column and then sweep round to mop up the rear. A favourite tactic, when the knights charged, was to open their ranks and let them through and then to cut down isolated knights as the horses tired.

For their part, the Crusaders learned to make better use of the infantry, employing cross-bowmen to protect the cavalry and pick off the Turks at a distance. They also learned a great deal about siege-warfare and castle-building, for these arts were much more advanced than in the West.

A Saracen or Turkish warrior, armed with scimitar, axe, dagger and short bow. His small round shield would give little protection against Frankish lances and crossbow bolts.

Top: a knight clad in chain mail. Below: a squire helps him to don the mailed shirt.

9

Fighting the Infidel

The most persistent Crusaders were the French—or Franks, as they were called at this time. The armies of the First Crusade came from southern France, from Normandy, from Flanders, and from the Norman possessions in southern Italy. Many Germans joined them and parties of Crusaders set out from Scotland and Scandinavia, but few Englishmen took part in the Holy War until the Third Crusade. For 200 years, the pattern was much the same; the bulk of the Crusaders were Franks, strongly backed at times by the Germans. Italian merchants arranged sea-transport, and contingents from other countries arrived from time to time. But the Crusader kingdoms were Frankish kingdoms, where the customs and language were French, modified by the climate of the East.

Each army was commanded by a king, a prince or a duke, to whose banners came numbers of nobles, bringing their own retainers. A landowner would equip himself, a number of knights, squires and foot-soldiers and attach his company to the forces of a greater lord. Armies of this kind were much weakened by jealousies and squabbles about rank.

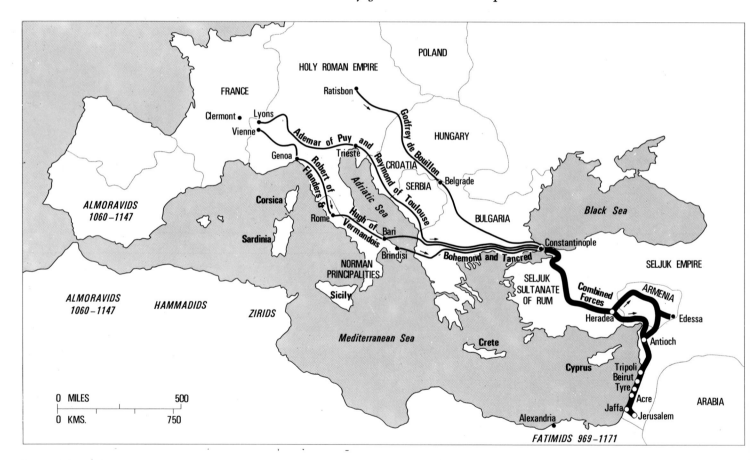

Attacking the Moors

Long before the First Crusade was launched, Christians had been fighting Arabs in Spain. The Arabs (Moors) had crossed from North Africa in the eighth century and had quickly conquered the entire country. They crossed the Pyrenees into France but were hurled back at the Battle of Tours by Charles Martel. For 300 years, Spain was torn by wars and anarchy but, by 1050, Castile and the Christian kingdoms of the north, which had somehow survived, began the reconquest. Christian knights went from all over Europe to fight the Arabs in Spain, and the Pope commanded Spaniards not to go on the Crusade but to fight the infidel at home. As in the East, the Arabs of Spain knew far more than the Christians about medicine, mathematics, science and astronomy.

The map above shows the routes taken on the First Crusade. The armies of the West gathered at three meeting-points, and marched overland at the pace of the waggons, covering about 20 miles a day. Only the Normans, who linked up with their cousins in southern Italy, made the sea-crossing to Greece. At Constantinople, the armies met and combined but, later, they split up again, owing to quarrels and greed.

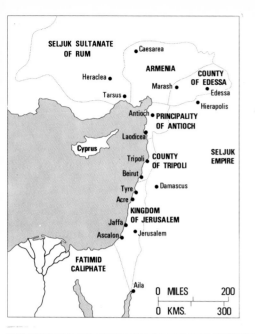

The Crusader States

The map shows the Crusader states set up by the Franks after the First Crusade captured Jerusalem in 1099. They were the Kingdom of Jerusalem, the County of Tripoli, the Principality of Antioch and the County of Edessa, the weakest, which was soon lost.

Together, the states were known as *Outremer*—"overseas". Like Israel today, Outremer could be attacked from the north, east and south; it was possession of the seaports that enabled the Christians to hold on for 200 years. The King of Jerusalem had an uneasy lordship over the other rulers, but his authority was often disputed or ignored.

Below: A French picture of the battle outside Antioch, a key city captured during the First Crusade, after a fearsome siege.

Henry I- Progress and Tragedy

Henry I loved money. When his father left him £5,000 in gold, he had it counted to make sure he had not been cheated; when his brother William Rufus was slain, he dashed to Winchester to seize the royal treasury before being crowned. His officials introduced the Exchequer which took its name from the chequered boards used to calculate taxes. So careful was the royal housekeeping that men said Henry counted the candle ends. But he ruled well. The kingdom was at peace; he won the English people's goodwill when he married Matilda, niece of Edgar the Atheling, his courts protected them against the barons and they willingly fought for him when he went to Normandy to defeat Robert Curthose. Henry's reign was prosperous and London's trade attracted immigrants from the continent; towns grew, abbeys and monasteries were built, Oxford university was born and the Cistercian monks arrived and began sheep-farming in desolate parts of the kingdom. One tragedy clouded the reign. Henry's son was drowned in the disaster of the White Ship, and there was none to succeed him, except a daughter, the Empress Matilda.

Building with stone

In the picture above you can see the tools used by medieval builders—axe, mallet, mason's hammer, plumbline, level, brace and bit, besides ladders, scaffolding and mechanical hoist. The Normans never baked bricks but used stone, mostly imported from Caen, and we hear of "ingenious machines for loading and unloading ships and for drawing cement and stone." The architect or master mason drew plans for the work, including drains which have since been mistaken for secret passages.

12th century picture of building the church at St Albans. The abbey, founded in Offa's reign, was rebuilt by the Normans. Henry I attended its dedication.

This Royal Writ has Henry I's seal attached. The "Lion of Justice", as he was called, sent his officials round the country, armed with writs like this to convene courts, control the sheriffs and hear cases in which the Crown was interested.

The King's nightmare: Henry dreams he is threatened by the barons. Many had supported Robert Curthose but Henry checked their power.

A tragic death

Henry had only two legitimate children, William and Matilda, who married the German Emperor. When Prince William was drowned, Henry was stunned with grief but, presently, he devised a plan to pass on the crown to his daughter. She was now a widow and he compelled the barons to swear an oath that they would accept her as their sovereign. They murmured but dared not refuse. To make Normandy safe, Henry married Matilda to Geoffrey of Anjou whose domains lay next to the duchy.

Prince William, sole heir to the throne, was returning from Normandy in the White Ship when a drunken helmsman ran the vessel on a rock. William got away in a small boat but turned back to save his half-sister. The boat capsized and all were drowned.

Stephen and the Proud Empress

When Henry I died, Matilda and her husband were in Anjou but, instead of hurrying to England, they decided to make sure of Normandy. At once, a rival appeared. Stephen of Blois, grandson of the Conqueror, claimed the throne and was crowned king. Matilda's half-brother, Robert of Gloucester, raised a revolt and, in 1139, Matilda herself arrived. Stephen was captured and, for a time, the Empress was triumphant. However, she behaved so arrogantly that the Londoners drove her out, Stephen was exchanged for Robert of Gloucester and, after that, her fortunes went downhill.

Eventually, she returned to Normandy but the civil war dragged on, chiefly because many barons were quarrelling over lands which had been lost or won. To Stephen, they gave neither respect nor obedience. Then appeared Matilda's son, Henry Plantagenet. Young, vigorous and already tremendously rich through his marriage to Eleanor of Aquitaine, he was accepted by Stephen as his adopted son and successor. In 1154, Stephen died and Henry became King of England and lord of an empire that stretched to the Pyrenees.

Matilda's seal (above): Matilda, also known as Maud, was sent as a child to be brought up in Germany and to marry the Emperor, Henry V.

Matilda's shield: widowed at 25, the Empress went to Normandy and married Geoffrey of Anjou, nicknamed "the Handsome", whose badge, a sprig of broom (*planta genista*), gave us the name Plantagenet.

A valiant but weak king

Stephen was brave, handsome and chivalrous. Once, when he could have captured Matilda, he let her go, saying he did not make war on a woman. He was Henry I's favourite nephew, the nobles regarded him as the first baron in the realm and he was popular with the common people. Yet, despite all his good qualities, Stephen was no ruler. He made such lavish promises and gifts that the barons lost respect for him and used him merely to enrich themselves.

Lawlessness in the land

Since Stephen was too easy-going to be ruthless or cruel, the barons soon saw they could do as they pleased without fear of punishment. They built illegal castles, recruited private armies and made war upon one another. They held prisoners to ransom, tortured them and put them to death. As always, the common people suffered, for when crops were burnt and cattle stolen, farming fell into ruins; when towns were looted and armed bands roamed the countryside, trade came to a standstill. "If three men came riding into a town," wrote a chronicler, "all the inhabitants fled." Men said openly that "Christ and his Saints slept".

Stephen of Blois, grandson of the Conqueror.

Stephen tried in vain to quell the barons and finish the war. Proof of his inability to rule like a king lies in the fact that, during his last two years, young Henry took over from him and won him more authority than he had ever known before. When Stephen's son died, he lost interest in the struggle and accepted Henry as his adopted son and successor.

Warlike as a man

Matilda's upbringing in Germany probably marked her character for life. Strictly reared, without love or warmth, she was married to a man years older than herself and accompanied him about the Empire to councils, battles and sieges. Red-haired, masterful and as warlike as a man, she next found herself a pawn in her father's dynastic game and married this time to a handsome boy.

In the civil war, she showed no tact or diplomacy, only a ferocious determination to win what she believed was her own kingdom. All the love in her fierce nature went to her son Henry and, in old age, when she lived piously in Rouen, she sent him much good advice on how to rule the stiff-necked English.

After Stephen's capture, Matilda entered London in triumph. Remembering perhaps that the Londoners had welcomed Stephen, she confiscated property, refused to grant the citizens their ancient rights, and tried to browbeat their leaders into handing over money. At this, the Londoners rioted (above) and forced Matilda to flee.

Stephen's seal: the royal seal was attached to grants of land, and the civil war went on for so long chiefly because of quarrels about land. Henry I, Stephen and Matilda all rewarded their friends with estates of their enemies, who, in turn, fought to win them back.

In 1142, Stephen besieged Matilda in Oxford Castle which stood by the river, almost surrounded by water. Frost set in and the garrison was starving when Matilda, aided by 4 knights dressed in white, slid down a rope from the battlements and escaped across the ice.

15

Early Castles

A castle was a private fortress belonging to a lord. It was a strong-point in a conquered land, a refuge from enemies, a dwelling-place and the centre of local government and justice. In this sense, castles were unknown in Britain until Norman times. The Normans and the French had become used to defending their lands with the help of wooden towers and when William the Conqueror took England, he secured his conquest by building these castles at key points all over the kingdom.

Local peasants were forced to excavate a ditch, throwing the earth inwards to form a mound (or *motte*) on which a wooden tower was erected. A fence, or palisade, protected the tower. Beyond the mound, but connected to it by extensions of palisade and ditch, was a good sized base-court or bailey for store-huts, kitchen and stables. This primitive fortress is known as the motte-and-bailey castle. Its advantage was that it could be erected quickly and cheaply and it was difficult for mailed knights to capture without plenty of infantry and archers. In England, a baron could not build a castle without the king's permission.

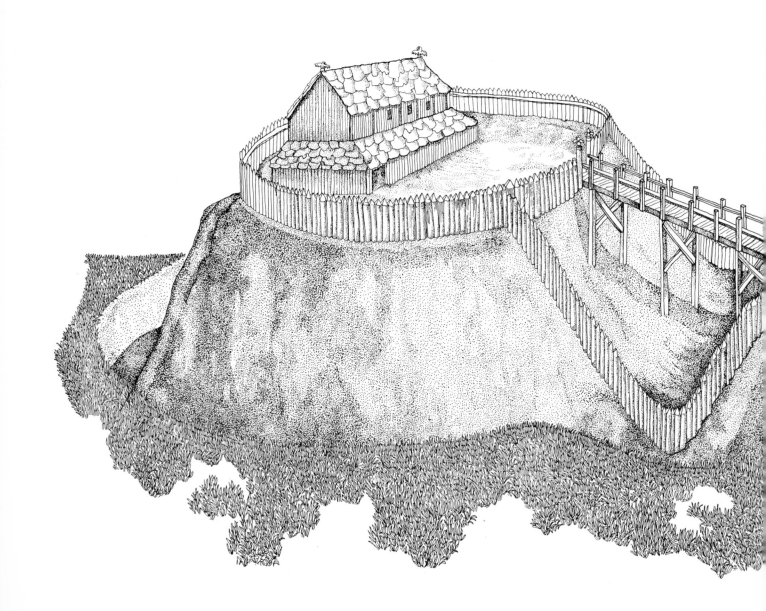

Remains of a *motte* (top left) with ditches and two baileys. As castles developed, a stone tower replaced the wooden one on the mound; stone walls, drawbridge, elaborate gatehouse, water-filled moat and outlying defence-work were gradually added.

A motte-and-bailey castle (below) similar to those which William erected all over England. The house often took the form of a tower with no entrance at ground-level; it would be draped with wet hides to reduce danger from fire attacks.

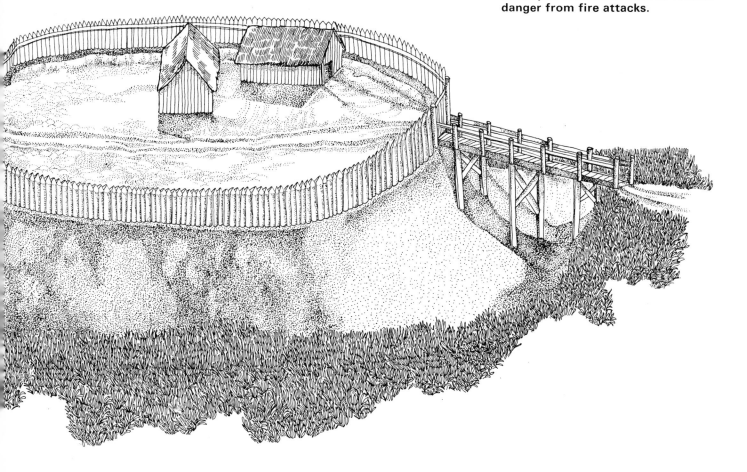

The First Plantagenet

When he came to the throne at the age of twenty-one, Henry II was the most powerful monarch in Europe. From his mother, he had inherited England and Normandy, from his father, Anjou, Maine and Touraine lying to the south of Normandy, and from his wife, Aquitaine, a huge province which stretched to the border of Spain. He also received the overlordship of Scotland, Wales, Brittany, Flanders and Boulogne.

This was not a kingdom but an empire with various laws, customs and languages, and it could only be held together by the personality of this young man who possessed such startling gifts and terrifying energy. It was never an English empire but a French one. Yet, because of Henry's interest and incessant travelling, because of the efficient men whom he chose to run the kingdom during his absences, England recovered from the civil war and prospered. The barons had to learn obedience and see their illegal castles destroyed; the ravaged countryside returned to the plough and English wool was made into cloth; trade increased, towns grew bigger, poetry, music and learning began to flourish.

Left: Geoffrey the Fair (or the Handsome) Count of Anjou, father of Henry II.

Above: Henry sails to England (1152) where he forces Stephen to accept him as his heir.

An Angevin at heart

Henry was an *Angevin*, that is, he came, on his father's side, from the Counts of Anjou, an ambitious hot-tempered breed. By taking Maine and part of Aquitaine, they enlarged their possessions and collided with the dukes of Normandy. But Henry I married his daughter Matilda to young Geoffrey the Handsome of Anjou, thus uniting the Angevin territories to England and Normandy—or so he hoped.

Eventually, Geoffrey's son was to inherit them but, at heart, Henry II remained an Angevin, more involved in France than in England.

Seal of Henry II, "the Law Giver", who laid down a system of law.

Order and justice

Henry II is one of the most fascinating characters in history. He had the build and strength of a wrestler and his explosive energy was the despair of his counsellors. Forever on the move through his vast dominions, he constantly had the whole paraphernalia of a medieval court trailing after him as he dashed ahead to a council or a battle. He was a good soldier, but if the same results could be gained by cunning, he preferred diplomacy to fighting.

His mind was like a blade. He was well-read, spoke several languages, never forgot a fact—or a grudge—and knew so much law that he was often asked to settle disputes between princes.

The barons, he knew, were the source of disorder and injustice in his realms, so he made himself the supreme fount of justice. He did not invent juries or royal writs or itinerant judges, but he drew these ideas together into a system of royal justice that was above the justice of the barons' courts.

The Common Law of England emerged and, by its side, statute law—the written laws which would be made later on by Parliaments. Order and justice in England—these were Henry's great achievements. In so much else, he failed—his empire broke up, the Church defeated him, and he died hated by his own wife and children.

Rebellion, intrigue and defeat

Henry married Eleanor of Aquitaine, divorced wife of Louis VII of France, and one of the greatest landowners in Europe. The marriage at once provoked the lasting enmity of France. Louis constantly encouraged the feuds of quarrelsome nobles in Henry's dominions, and he nursed the rebellions of Henry's sons. In 1173, for instance, young Henry, the eldest son, fled to Louis and was joined by his brothers, Richard and Geoffrey. Together, they and the discontented barons hatched a full-scale rebellion, but Henry mastered them and forced them to beg for peace.

However, the intrigues went on and, when Louis died, Richard made a pact with his son Philip Augustus. In 1189, they suddenly invaded the Angevin dominions from two sides; Henry, ill and caught with only a few troops, put up a fierce resistance but was forced to accept humiliating terms.

When he saw the name of John, his youngest and best-loved son, among those who had headed the rebellion, he gave way to despair, crying, "Shame, shame on a conquered King". Three days later he was dead.

A rounded bastion (left) of the 12th century wall of Poitiers which was besieged several times during the rebellions of Henry's sons. In any quarrel with their father, they could always count on the King of France.

Louis VIII of France (1137–1180), first husband of Eleanor of Aquitaine and a Crusader who became obsessed by religion. He kept up ceaseless intrigues against Henry II because the Angevin empire threatened the kingdom of France.

More French than English

Although Henry II inherited vast possessions, he never rested content. At his accession, he found that the Scots had recovered their independence, Wales had thrown off Norman rule, Aquitaine was in chaos and several vassals had forgotten their obligations. Henry put his empire to rights. He defeated the Scots and, later, made William the Lion pay homage for his kingdom. He subdued Wales and partly conquered Ireland.

But France took most of his attention, for his lands there were greater than those of the King of France. The Duke of Brittany had to acknowledge Henry's overlordship, and he married his son Geoffrey to the Duke's heiress; his son Richard subdued Aquitaine; the Counts of Boulogne, Flanders and Ponthieu agreed to resume their feudal dues, the Count of Toulouse paid homage, and a district of France was gained when young Henry married the French King's daughter.

Henry's three daughters were married to Alfonso of Castile, Henry the Lion of Saxony, and William II of Sicily. Yet, at the summit of his power, Henry's sons rebelled and when he died, his empire began to break up.

Left: Eleanor of Aquitaine, the fiery-tempered queen.

Above: The dying Henry learns that his son John has joined the rebels.

A clever, influential queen

It is said that Eleanor of Aquitaine decided to marry the masterful young Henry when she first saw him at her husband's Court. At all events, Louis VII divorced her and, for a time, she and Henry were happy and had a large family. Gradually, love turned to indifference and then to hatred. Eleanor returned to Aquitaine to become the centre of a brilliant court. Later, she supported her sons' rebellion and was going to join them, disguised as a man, when she was captured. Henry imprisoned her for sixteen years but, after his death, she had great influence over her sons, Richard and John. As Regent, she helped to frustrate John's plotting with the King of France, made Richard forgive his brother and, in her old age, crushed a rising by Arthur of Brittany against John. She died, over eighty, in 1204, one of the cleverest and most passionate women in history.

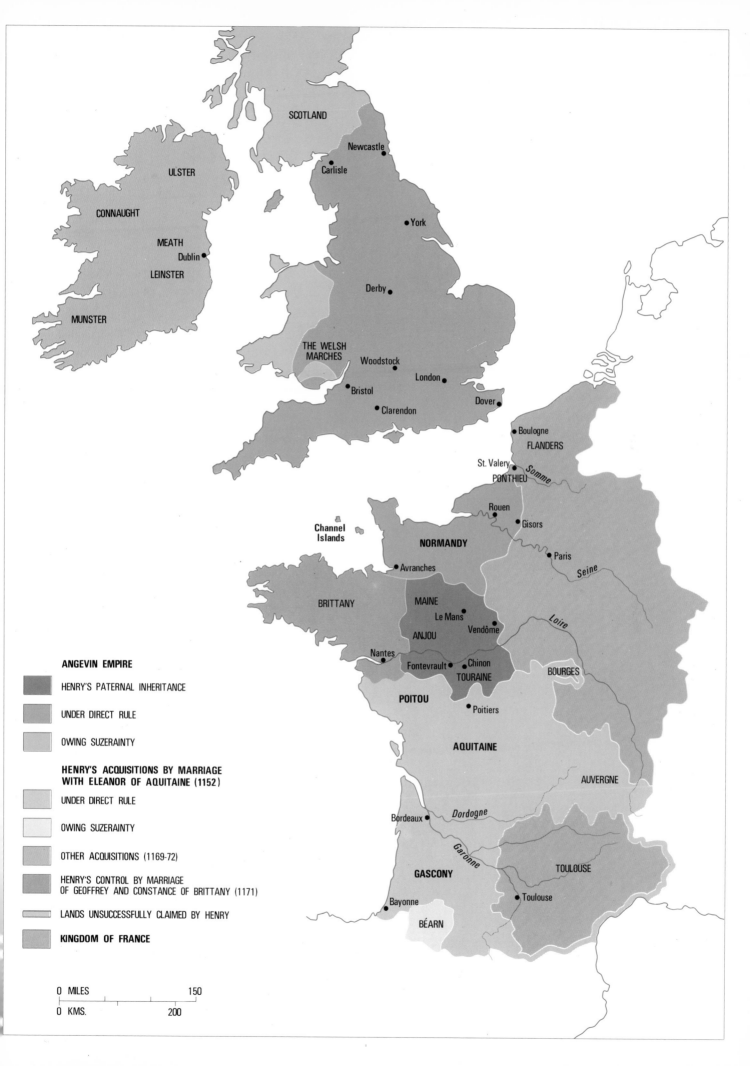

SCOTLAND

Newcastle

Carlisle

ULSTER

CONNAUGHT

MEATH
Dublin
LEINSTER

MUNSTER

York

Derby

THE WELSH
MARCHES

Woodstock

London

Bristol

Clarendon

Dover

Boulogne

FLANDERS

St. Valery

Somme

PONTHIEU

Channel
Islands

Rouen

Gisors

Paris

NORMANDY

Seine

Avranches

MAINE

BRITTANY

Le Mans

Vendôme

Loire

ANJOU

Nantes

Fontevrault

Chinon

BOURGES

TOURAINE

POITOU

Poitiers

AQUITAINE

AUVERGNE

Bordeaux

Dordogne

Garonne

GASCONY

TOULOUSE

Bayonne

Toulouse

BÉARN

ANGEVIN EMPIRE

HENRY'S PATERNAL INHERITANCE

UNDER DIRECT RULE

OWING SUZERAINTY

**HENRY'S ACQUISITIONS BY MARRIAGE
WITH ELEANOR OF AQUITAINE (1152)**

UNDER DIRECT RULE

OWING SUZERAINTY

OTHER ACQUISITIONS (1169-72)

HENRY'S CONTROL BY MARRIAGE
OF GEOFFREY AND CONSTANCE OF BRITTANY (1171)

LANDS UNSUCCESSFULLY CLAIMED BY HENRY

KINGDOM OF FRANCE

0 MILES 150

0 KMS. 200

The Murder of Becket

Through the Middle Ages, the authority of the Pope grew so strong that he was able to interfere in State affairs all over Europe. In England, the Church increased its power during the civil wars of Stephen's reign because the King's authority was much weakened. Henry II was not anti-clerical; on the contrary, he was a devout believer who from time to time suffered agonies of repentance for his sins, but he did not like the Church encroaching upon his rights to dispense justice.

In particular, he disliked the Church Courts dealing with land cases and, while he accepted the Church's right to try its own wrong-doers, everyone knew that Church punishments were less severe than those imposed by lay courts. Criminals could escape the death penalty by mumbling a few Latin words to prove they were "clerks". It was in order to limit the privileges of the Church Courts that Henry persuaded Becket to accept the post of Archbishop of Canterbury, and when he appeared to have betrayed his earthly master, a quarrel broke out that led to the murder of the Archbishop. After this, Henry had no hope of defeating the Church.

Two scenes from the life of Thomas Becket in a 14th century psalter. At the top, the King hands Becket a letter nominating him Archbishop of Canterbury; by this masterstroke, Henry thought that the affairs of both State and Church would now be in the capable hands of his friend. In the second picture, the Archbishop dares to oppose the King.

A monk and a nun in the stocks. Church wrongdoers usually received mild punishments—fasting, a whipping or a spell in the stocks.

From courtier to martyr

Thomas Becket was born in London, the son of well-to-do Norman parents; he was educated in England and Paris and was taken into the household of Archbishop Theobald. He travelled, studied law in Italy and became bosom-friend of Henry of Anjou.

When Henry became King, Becket was made Chancellor, the most powerful layman in the kingdom. Disliked by the nobility for his arrogance, he lived in magnificence that outshone the King's own court. Then, in 1161, Theobald died and, by King Henry's direction, Becket was consecrated as his successor. The appointment was a scandal, in that he was a courtier and was ordained priest only one day before his elevation.

At once, an astonishing change came over Becket; he resigned the Chancellorship, lived in devout poverty and opposed the King at every turn. So fierce was their argument that he fled into exile but, no sooner had the Pope patched up the quarrel and Becket returned to Canterbury, than he excommunicated the bishops who had sided with Henry during his absence.

Proud, obstinate and narrow-minded, he seemed to offer himself for martyrdom, for he must have known how Henry would react. The famous Angevin temper blazed out and four knights slipped away from Normandy, crossed to England and told Becket point-blank that he must come to heel or suffer the consequence. Icily, he defied them and they hacked him to death in his own cathedral.

The death of the Archbishop (opposite), from a panel on Henry IV's tomb at Canterbury. St Thomas's shrine became a rich and immensely popular place of pilgrimage.

The Story of Scotland

From Anglo-Saxon times, the kings of England always considered that they were overlords of Scotland. Ties between the countries became closer in Malcolm Canmore's reign, when, in 1070, he married Margaret, sister of Edgar Atheling. She brought English friends and priests with her, and her three sons, Edgar, Alexander and David, all kings, felt themselves as much English as Scottish.

In the twelfth century, many English nobles (such as the Bruces and the Balliols) obtained lands in Scotland while keeping their estates in England. This Anglo-Norman influence strengthened the authority of the Scottish king, but did not stop the English kings from pressing their overlordship claims, nor did the Scottish monarchs appear to feel humiliated by being treated as vassals.

This phase came to an end when William the Lion, who sided with Henry II's sons, was captured and made to do homage and surrender hostages and castles as security for his good behaviour. In 1189, Richard I, raising money for the Crusade, released him from these obligations for 10,000 marks.

David I (1124–1153) and his grandson, Malcolm IV (1153–1165), from the 14th century Kelso Charter. In Stephen's reign, David seized three English counties but was later defeated. Malcolm was William the Lion's brother.

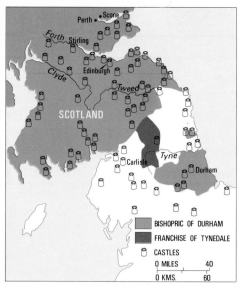

The Scottish border area, for centuries a battle-ground for Scots and English. Both sides built castles and Carlisle, Norham, Roxburgh and Berwick were some of the strongholds that dominated the area.

Plundering the borderlands

The old kingdoms of Northumbria and Cumbria once lay across the modern border, but, by 1200, the frontier was more or less fixed. The Solway in the west and the Tweed in the east were linked by the Cheviot Hills. On either side, people alike in ancestry and upbringing, lived hard, rearing cattle and sheep for their flesh and wool.

Border strife was rare during the period of Anglo-Norman settlement but, after Edward I claimed over-lordship and war broke out in 1296, the borderland was crossed and recrossed by enemy forces. For two centuries, the area was ravaged by armies who lived by plunder and ransom, while border lords, such as the Percys, the Nevilles and the Douglases, carried on private wars like gangsters.

The round keep of Conisborough Castle (1180).

Peasants reaping a meagre harvest. In the border country, there was not a great deal of arable land and continuous warfare led to depopulation.

Queen (later, Saint) Margaret arrives in Scotland, 1068, to marry Malcolm Canmore.

Castles and huts

In the thirteenth century, life in Scotland was crude and harsh. The baron's earth and timber castle was now being rebuilt with stone walls and a great tower or *donjon* in place of the old wooden tower, yet it was still a draughty, comfortless place in which to live; windows were un-glazed, food was cooked outside, and smoke from a central fireplace eddied about the room. But this was luxury compared with the huts, roofed and walled with turf, in which the peasants lived and slept alongside their cattle.

Towns, trade and guilds

Numbers of burghs or towns were coming into existence, many of them close to some great monastery or castle, or on a river or beside a natural harbour. A burgh consisted of a main street of thatched wooden houses with a stone church, castle and guild-hall, the meeting-place of the Merchant Guild (an exclusive society) which organised the trade of the burgh. Business was done round the market-cross, where strange merchants had to display their wares to the burgesses, giving first choice to the Guild members. It was they who governed the burgh in accordance with the rights or "liberties" granted by the king, a bishop or a baron.

The birth of a nation

At about this time, a curious change occurred: Scotland's mixture of peoples—Norman barons, English-speaking traders, Lowland farmers and Gaelic-speaking herdsmen—began to think of themselves as Scots. They became a nation.

Early Scots Heroes

The great struggle between England and Scotland followed a long period of peace and friendship. Alexander III, after a reign of nearly forty years, died in 1286, when his horse carried him over a cliff; he left no sons but a grand-daughter, the little "Maid of Norway", who died on the way to Scotland.

The six Guardians of the Realm, perplexed by the claims to the throne of no fewer than thirteen nobles, appealed to Edward I of England for a judgment. He agreed to hear the claims at Norham Castle on condition that the successful candidate would pay homage to him for the whole of Scotland.

The claims were complicated and, in the end, Edward awarded the crown to John Balliol, a descendant of William the Lion's brother. This was acceptable to the Scots until Edward put pressure on the docile Balliol and treated him as though he were a mere baron holding an estate by permission of his English overlord. At length, Balliol refused to support Edward in a war against France and made an alliance with the French King. This was the excuse that Edward wanted, and in 1296 he invaded Scotland.

William Wallace, the first Scottish patriot to take up arms against the English oppressors.

Guerrilla leader of genius

William Wallace, a Scottish knight, killed an English soldier who insulted him as he was riding home. His wife was murdered in retaliation and Wallace, now an outlaw, raised a force of farmers and peasants (the nobles ignored him) to harass the occupying forces.

Wallace, a guerrilla leader of genius, was highly successful until he made the mistake of fighting the English in a pitched battle at Falkirk. He was defeated and fled to France but, on his return, he was betrayed by a fellow-Scot to the English and hanged in London. The four quarters of his body were shown in Scottish towns but they aroused, not fear, but a fierce spirit of patriotism.

Robert Bruce (1306–1329) with his wife who, like Balliol's wife (far right) wears his coat of arms on her dress.

Robert Bruce's victory

After Wallace's death, Robert Bruce, grandson of the claimant, made a bid for the throne and had himself crowned at Scone. The English scattered his puny force and compelled him to take refuge in the Highlands, but he gradually built up an army, captured the English-held castles and defeated Edward II at Bannockburn in 1314. He continued to harry the northern counties until the treaty of Northampton (1328) brought an end to the strife.

Above and opposite: John Balliol (1292–1296), the successful candidate, does homage to Edward I for the kingdom of Scotland.

"Empty-coat"

Edward I went to great pains to make it clear that John Balliol was the rightful King of Scotland. He made it equally clear that he was his rightful overlord, until poor Balliol became known as "Toom Tabard"—"Empty coat", meaning there was no man inside his tunic. When Balliol at last defied Edward, the English King defeated him at Dunbar and made him come to London.

The Progress of Medicine

In the Middle Ages, it was dangerous for scholars and students to question old beliefs and to seek new knowledge. If they did so, they risked accusations of witchcraft and heresy, the dread crime of daring to question the Church. In no subject was this more true than in medicine. The knowledge built up by the Greeks had been lost or had been acquired by the Arabs and, although travellers and Crusaders knew that Arab doctors were far more advanced than Westerners, it was risky to say so.

Illness was due to sin and to devils who could affect, say, the head or the stomach; the priest was therefore more important than the doctor. In any case, remedies were based on superstition and fixed theories, often absurd, about the body's working; the nastier the remedy the better—severe bleeding, boiling oil, medicines containing toads, snakes, powdered skulls, gems and even gold. The only worthwhile knowledge was of herbs.

Since the Church banned dissection, there was little knowledge of anatomy; surgery was carried out by barbers. Lack of antiseptics meant that any operation was likely to be fatal.

albule oculorum sic exaauntur;

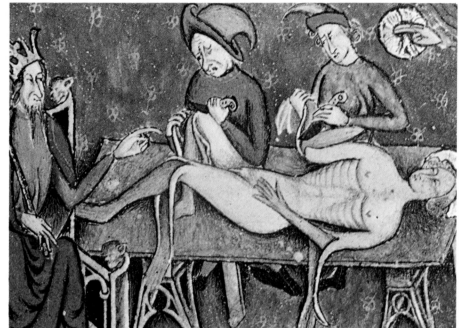

The human body

Surgery was regarded as inferior to medicine and, since the Church forbade dissection and the Arabs' religion forbade study of anatomy, there was only the vaguest knowledge of the human body. Men believed that blood was produced in the liver and that two kinds of blood moved separately up and down the body. There was no way to stop arterial bleeding. In England, surgery was left to barbers but there were schools of surgery from the tenth century at Salerno, Italy, and later in Bologna and Paris.

Flaying alive: although dissection was banned by the Church for the study of anatomy, tortures such as this were practised.

An early example of accurate observation of nature: this 13th century drawing of the elephant which the King of France gave to Henry III was made by Matthew Paris, a learned monk of St Albans. Rare animals, such as giraffes, lions, elephants and monkeys, excited much interest in the Middle Ages and for many years there was a royal menagerie at the Tower of London.

An eye operation (opp.): the surgeon's calling was a dangerous one; if his lord died, he would be put to death.

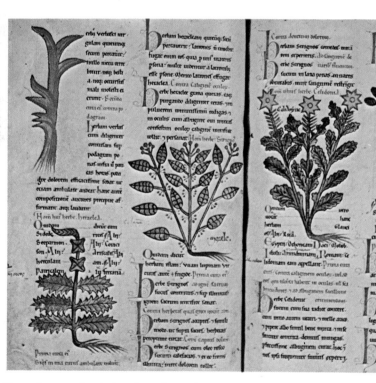

Page from a herb-book written in Latin. Holly leaves were used to make medicinal tea, nettle-leaves relieved toothache, coltsfoot leaves and flowers made a cough mixture and hawksweed cleansed the blood.

Healing with herbs

Today's medicines are only chemical versions of the healing properties of herbs, and this knowledge, kept alive by monks and "wise women", was the only useful medical aid in the Middle Ages. Every monastery, castle and town had its herb garden or Physick Garden, and a monk or herb-man would boil, crush and distil the herb crop into potions, liquors and ointments.

Stomach troubles were widespread, probably due to infected water and putrid meat and fish, and herbs which were specially good for stomach-ache included wormwood, yarrow, centaury, gentian, parsley and sage. Sage was such an all-round tonic for the liver, blood, brain, stomach, nerves and heart that a medieval proverb asked, "Why should a man die whilst sage grows in his garden?"

Other useful herbs were arnica which healed cuts, St John's wort for rheumatism and sore throats, valerian for heart trouble, camomile for swellings, mistletoe to improve the blood and Alpine Lady's mantle to stop bleeding. Garlic was supposed to give courage in battle, the poisonous hemlock and henbane could be carefully prepared to cure fainting spells, cholera, earache and toothache. As a rule, just one part of a plant was known to be useful—the root, the leaves, seeds or flower-head.

Primitive Justice

In Anglo-Saxon times most crimes were punished by making the wrong-doer pay a sum of money (*wergild*) to the victim—three shillings for wounding a freeman, for example. Some crimes, like murder and arson, were so wicked as to be "bootless", which meant they could not be wiped out by a money payment and the criminal was put to death.

William the Conqueror abolished the death penalty and replaced it by mutilation or blinding, but Henry I restored it, and death became the normal punishment for all "felonies". Felonies were crimes which included murder, rape, and "grand larceny" (theft of anything worth one shilling or more). Minor crimes included brawling and petty larceny (theft of goods worth less than a shilling).

After the Conquest, the barons dealt with many offenders in their own manorial courts, a power which Henry II took steps to weaken. At this time, a man could only be brought to court by his accuser or by the victim's relations and, in many cases, his guilt or innocence would only be revealed through the Ordeal, the Oath or the Combat.

A 17th century ducking-stool, a relic of Ordeal by Water in medieval times, when the accused was thrown bound into a pond or river; if he sank, he was innocent, if he floated, guilty. In either case, his chances were not very bright.

Trial by Ordeal: the accused had to carry a red-hot iron bar three paces or pick a stone out of boiling water. If the hand blistered, the man was guilty.

Guilty or innocent

From early times men believed in signs and portents. The stars, the flight of birds, the intestines of a sacrificed animal would help the king's advisers to solve difficulties and make decisions.

In the Middle Ages, people believed that God, or Divine Providence, would send a sign to show whether an accused person was guilty or innocent. Trial by Ordeal, therefore, was a solemn ceremony, with the iron bar or water heated in church and the priest supervising the bandaging and unwrapping of the hand. He was present when the accused was thrown into the river and, in Trial by Morsel, placed the morsel of bread in the accused's mouth. If the iron did not burn, if the bread did not choke and if the water did not reject the accused, it was clear that he was innocent.

Ordeal by Combat, introduced by the Normans, was a battle to decide a dispute between nobles; since God supported the righteous, victory would go to the man who was in the right. This form of trial obviously gave a strong man an advantage and it became customary to hire champions to do the fighting.

Another way of deciding a difficult case was for a man to get a body of men to swear on oath the truth of the matter, calling on God to punish them if they lied.

Ordeal by Combat (opposite): two champions armed with the special axes carried in these contests, are about to decide right from wrong.

How our Laws Began

Henry II, a Frenchman, gave England her system of law. He did not invent royal justice or the jury system, for these went far back into Saxon times; what he did was to draw old ideas together into a regular system and, above all, to make royal justice (the king's court and the king's judges) superior to the justice handed out by the unruly barons in their own private courts.

Only the king had the right to summon a jury and Henry did not grant it to private courts, but only to those who asked for justice in the royal courts. It gradually became clear that a man could get better justice from trial by jury than from a baron or his steward. Travelling judges—"justices in eyre"—moved round the country to hear cases in the shire courts which were thus taken away from the control of local lords.

In this way, justice was the same everywhere, and a Common Law, the same for all men in all places, came into existence. Henry II laid the foundations of the English Common Law which, changed and adapted through the centuries, has become the law in America and in the British Commonwealth.

A judge in his robes: educated in a monastery school, he probably studied law in London and Paris.

The pillory was used to punish cheats, brawlers and petty thieves, who were mocked and pelted with rubbish.

Thumbscrew to extract confessions. The prisoner's hands were tied behind his back and when the instrument was placed over both thumbs, the screw was tightened.

Trial by jury

Jurymen of Henry II's time were picked, not to give a verdict after listening to evidence, but because they were the likeliest persons to know what was the truth. On oath, they would tell the judge what they knew about the case. As yet, there was no prosecutor, no defence counsel.

Nobody could be tried by jury against his will but there were ways of "encouraging" him—he might be kept in prison or made to suffer *peine forte et dure* ("suffering strong and hard") which meant that heavy stones and iron weights were laid on his body until he agreed to stand trial. He might bravely suffer this agony, because all the goods and lands of a convicted person were forfeited.

Avoiding prison

Prison was otherwise used only for men awaiting trial and for those who had not paid fines; convictions were few because the police system was primitive and not many criminals got caught. A wrong-doer would find it easy to escape from the village lock-up or he might claim "benefit of Clergy". This meant that if he could read a verse from Psalm 51, he had proved that he was of the clergy and therefore able to escape the harsher penalties of the law. Another criminal might take sanctuary in a church where he could stay unharmed for forty days. Outlaws, supposed to be killed on sight, usually managed to stay free.

The Court of King's Bench in Henry III's reign. You can see the judges, clerks of the Court, officials, a juryman or witness taking the oath and a line of accused persons.

Loyal Servants

Medieval government, peace, law and order depended upon the king. It mattered little whether he was personally good, as long as he was strong enough to control the barons and see that justice was done in the land. But even a strong king like Henry I or Henry II needed servants to help him to rule.

As he moved about the kingdom, he was accompanied by the *Curia Regis* (the King's Court) — a body of officials including the Justiciar (chief officer of the realm), the Chancellor (royal secretary), the Treasurer, the Chamberlain (master of the household) and the Marshal (organiser of the armed forces). These ministers were entirely dependent upon the king's favour, for he could destroy them at will or reward them, chiefly with guardianship of estates and custody of royal wards (noble orphans). There was also much to be gained in gifts from persons who wanted some favour or royal grant.

Serving the king was nevertheless fraught with danger, since an official was bound to arouse the enmity of the barons and, in times of war, it was easy to back the wrong side and to end up losing estates and perhaps life itself.

William Marshal—poor knight

The career of William Marshal illustrates the ups and downs in the life of a royal servant. Born in Stephen's reign, William was the son of John the Marshal, a ruffianly adventurer who, in the civil war, acquired lands and a noble wife.

As a young man, William went off to make his fortune in the wars in France. He was so poor that, after being knighted, he had to sell his ceremonial mantle to buy a horse.

In battles and tournaments, he won not only plunder and ransoms but a reputation for all the knightly virtues. This seems strange when we read that he would linger on the edge of a mêlée until the contestants were tired and then take several prisoners!

Royal tutor

Eleanor of Aquitaine, who loved chivalrous young men, helped his career and Henry II made him tutor-in-arms to his heir. When this young Henry rebelled, William found himself fighting against the King, but Henry pardoned him. He stayed with the old King to the end and had just fought Richard, when Henry died.

Earl of Pembroke

Richard I generously confirmed his father's promise that William should marry Isobel, heiress of the Earl of Pembroke, and, thus, the once-penniless knight became lord of vast estates in England, Wales, Ireland and Normandy.

During Richard's absence on a Crusade, William was one of the kingdom's principal officers. He

William Marshal victorious: a knight could win fame and fortune by his skill in the French tournaments.

opposed John's disloyal behaviour and he was with Richard when he died in France. Once again, William's reputation stood him in good stead, for John respected him and, in return, William stuck to him and fought for him against the barons.

Regent and guardian

At John's death William gave his allegiance to 9-year-old Henry III and, as Regent, led the army that defeated the French at the Battle of Lincoln. In 1219, the valiant old warrior-courtier-statesman died — he had lived through five reigns and had loyally served four kings.

The face of William Marshal, 2nd Earl of Pembroke, loyal servant to four kings of England.

Richard - the Absent King

Richard the Lion Heart has always been England's hero-king. Handsome, athletic, a champion in hand-to-hand combat and a master of siege-craft, he was generous towards his enemies and even to those who had wronged him. Yet, for all his courage and gallantry, he was unfitted to be a king. He had no sense of responsibility and cared nothing for England and its people, except as a source of money for his wars.

Soon after his accession, he left for the Holy Land where he won renown against Saladin, quarrelled with all his allies, failed to take Jerusalem and was captured on the way home and held to ransom for a year. He returned to England merely to equip himself for a war in France against Philip Augustus and, when he died besieging an obscure castle, he had spent only six months of his ten-year reign in England.

Despite his great reputation, he achieved very little and made no lasting conquests or contribution to his country, except the granting of town-charters. But, though he taxed and neglected them, the English loved their absentee hero and willingly paid the vast sum demanded for his ransom.

Richard arrested (above): the travellers had excited suspicion when Richard's page tendered a gold coin to pay for food in the market and was seen to be carrying his master's gloves, a luxury worn only by nobles.

Richard's disguise removed (right): taken prisoner by Leopold, Duke of Austria, the English king was handed over to the Emperor and remained a captive for many months.

Ransom for a king

When the Crusaders captured Acre, the Austrians hung their flag on the wall alongside the English flag, at which Richard had it torn down and trampled upon. Breathing vengeance, Leopold of Austria went home. More than a year later, Richard set out for England, deciding to risk crossing Leopold's territory, because the route across France was held by his enemy, Philip Augustus. He had reached Vienna in disguise, when his page's lavish spending aroused suspicion and the travellers were arrested.

Leopold gleefully shut Richard up in a castle but he soon had to hand over the prisoner to his overlord, the Emperor Henry VI. For some time, the regents in England were uncertain where Richard was held, and this probably gave rise to the story of his faithful minstrel Blondel, going from castle to castle, playing his harp until he heard an answering voice from inside the walls. The English had to pay the first instalment of a huge ransom before their hero was released.

Richard meets his end

Richard laid seige to Chaluz Castle when its owner, the Count of Limoges, refused to hand over some treasure. While reconnoitring the defences, Richard was struck by an arrow fired by Bertrand de Gurdun. The castle fell and de Gurdun was brought before the dying king to whom he declared that he fired the arrow because Richard had slain his father and brothers. Richard forgave him but, when he died, the soldiers flayed de Gurdun alive and hanged him.

Philip Augustus (left), Richard's one-time ally and implacable enemy. He aimed to break up the Angevin empire and win back Normandy.

An archer (right) draws his bow with his hands and feet. Richard was probably killed by a bolt from a crossbow fired from the shoulder.

Warfare, weapons and armour

In Richard I's day, the key figure in warfare was the armoured knight, clad from head to foot in chain mail and mounted on a heavily-built war-horse, a most valuable creature specially trained for battle.

By the late twelfth century, the Norman helmet, with its *nasal* or nose-piece, had been replaced by a flat or round-topped helm completely covering the face, apart from an eye-slit and breathing holes.

The shield had become smaller and less kite-shaped, and it bore the owner's badge. His weapons were lance, sword and battle-axe or mace.

Foot-soldiers were regarded as of little account, though necessary for camp-duties, siege-work and all the lowly tasks of warfare.

Chivalry, the glory of the charge and the profitable business of ransoms were reserved for the nobility and knights.

The lower the rank, the less protection, so foot soldiers wore little in the way of armour beyond a basin-shaped helmet and a leather jacket or padded tunic.

During the Crusades and in

Richard leads his army against the French during the Battle of Gisors, 1198. He routed Philip and drove him through the town in which, 10 years before, they had sworn Crusaders' oaths of friendship.

siege-warfare, the knights came to realise the importance of infantry, especially archers; crossbowmen became essential, because their heavy bolts flew farther and were much more deadly than arrows from the short bow used at this time.

The Battle

Feudal society was organised for war. The main condition of holding land was military service and, in theory, countries like England and France could put thousands of knights in the field. However, unpaid military service lasted for only forty days and this caused difficulties on long campaigns, especially overseas.

So, by the twelfth and thirteenth centuries, it became convenient for kings and great lords to make up their armies with mercenaries—landless knights, younger sons and professional soldiers who fought for pay and plunder. Fighting became a way of life for these men and for many nobles in Normandy and France.

Campaigning began in the spring and lasted until autumn, with armies marching and besieging castles. Pitched battles were seldom fought but there was a great deal of skirmishing, and plundering of towns. Exchanges of prisoners were constantly arranged, for it was more profitable to capture an important enemy than to kill him. The mailed knight was so well protected that very few were killed in battle: neglected wounds and camp-fever killed more men than swords and lances.

Knights and their war-horses: fed on oats and very expensive to keep, these great horses, called *destriers*, were trained for war and were used for nothing else. For everyday use, the knights rode a *palfrey*.

Conway Castle built by Edward I. Rounded towers deflected missiles and enabled defenders to fire downwards and sideways at attackers at the base of a long curtain wall.

Preparing for battle

The knight's suit of mail was made of hundreds of small steel rings, and was expertly made to measure by an armourer. First, with a squire's help, the *chausses* or mailed leggings were pulled on; next came a padded vest, the *aketon*, and, over it, the long-sleeved mailed shirt, the *hauberk*, which reached to the knees. On his head, the knight wore a skull-cap beneath his *coif*, a mailed hood that covered the ears and neck. His flat-topped helm, heavy to wear and difficult to breathe in, was not put on until just before the battle, when he slipped his hands into mailed gloves at his wrists.

The mounted knight

His horse, sometimes given protective mail on its head and chest, carried a heavy saddle made of wood and leather, with a back-piece to provide support during the charge. Mounted, the knight let his shield hang loose from its neck-strap while he took the reins in his left hand and clamped the butt of his lance under his right armpit. He was now ready to charge.

At close quarters, he dropped the lance, slipped his left arm through the shield loops and grasped the handgrip, as he drew his sword. His horse, trained to stand the din of battle, would move in response to his voice, knees and spurs.

Knights usually served a great lord whose land was divided into so many "knights' fees", each fee having to support a knight who followed his lord and the king.

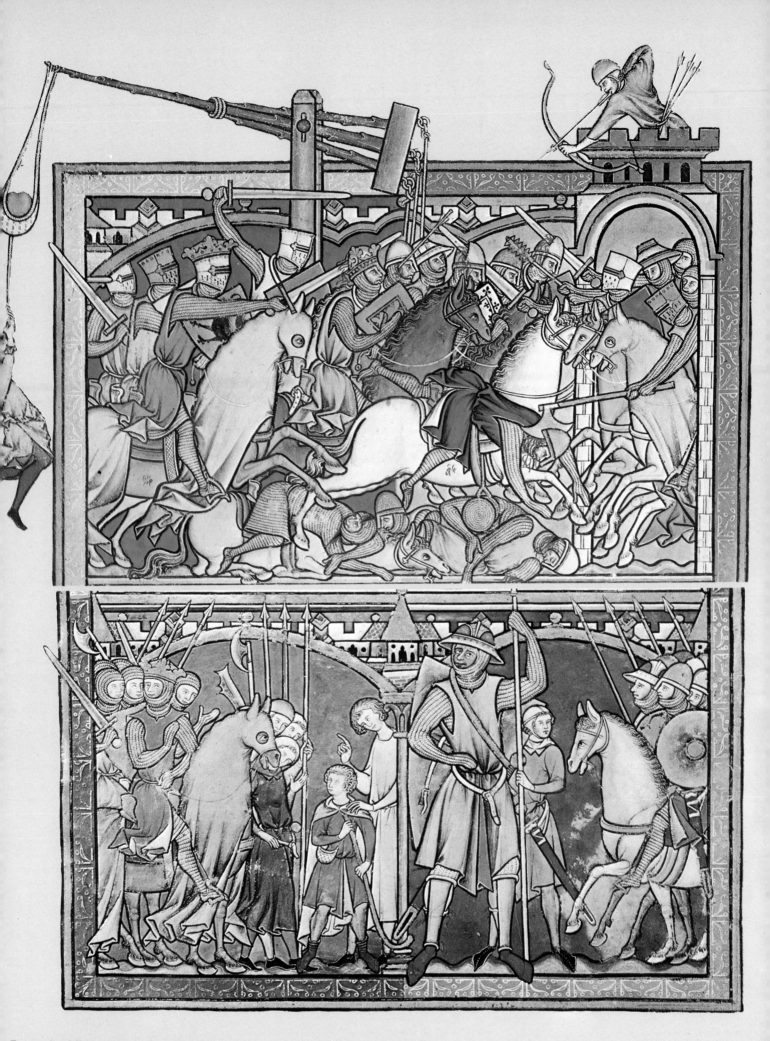

From the 13th century Maciejowski Psalter: the ingredients of warfare—cavalry, infantry, archers and siege machines. On the left, a man struggles to fire a trebuchet, a missile-throwing machine.

The Tournament

Tournaments first made their appearance in France and, by the twelfth century, were so popular that knights would travel great distances to fight alongside their overlord or, as freelances, to offer their services to some great baron. These early tournaments were mock-battles in which men were killed, wounded and taken prisoner, so that large sums could be won in ransoms. William Marshal, hero of some 500 tournaments, made his fortune in this way.

A prince or wealthy lord would proclaim the rules and provide the prizes. On a given date, the sides assembled, each wearing distinctive badges on shields and surcoats, and the battle took place all over the countryside, with spectators watching the sport and sometimes joining in.

Several Popes, who felt that knights would be better employed as Crusaders, tried to ban tournaments, and both Richard I and Henry III frowned on them, because gatherings of armed nobles could threaten a king's authority. At times, a mock-battle became all too serious, as in France in 1273, when many contestants were killed in "the little battle of Châlons".

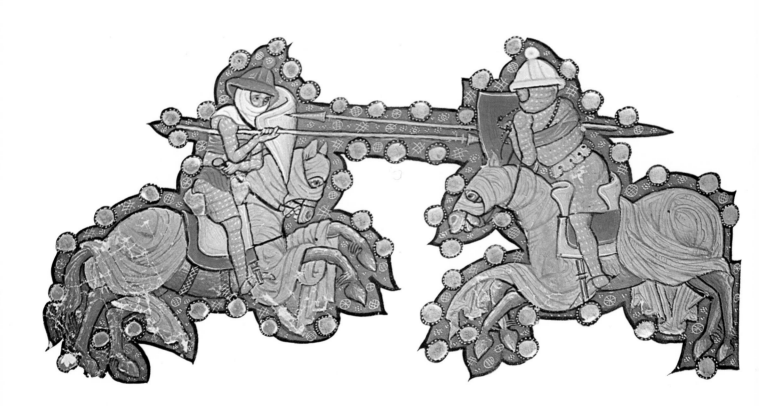

From mock-battles to jousts

Edward I brought in some new rules to make tournaments safer. A knight could bring no more than three squires with him, no sharp weapons were allowed, the taking of prisoners for ransom was banned and a panel of stewards strictly enforced the rules.

Jousts eventually took the place of mock-battles; a joust was held in the "lists", an enclosure with a fence or "tilt" down the middle. The two contestants charged along either side of it, each aiming his lance at the other's shield.

Colourful, extravagant tournaments were modelled on legends of King Arthur's court, with knights jousting as champions of ladies who watched the sport from stands and gave favours to the winners.

An engagement between two knights in an early tournament (above); they carry real lances, for the tournament trained men for actual warfare.

A 12th century picture (opposite) of knights jousting in front of ladies of the court; the knights wear chain mail and carry real weapons; there is no tilt separating them, for this is a tournament fought over a wide area, as well as beneath stands.

Ireland, the Land of Kings

Between the conversion of Ireland by St Patrick and the arrival of the Norsemen, the history of Ireland is almost a blank. We know that the monasteries were rich and learned, and that groups of tribes ruled by so-called kings gave a shadowy allegiance to the King of Tara, a sacred place surmounted by ancient earthworks. The tribes kept up perpetual warfare against one another, yet they possessed so little military organisation that, in the ninth century, the Vikings found it easy to strike where they pleased.

They first attacked near Dublin in 795 and soon no corner of Ireland was safe. The great monastic school at Clonmacnoise was sacked and Irish scholars fled to the continent. The foreigners settled at strongly-defended points which they used as ports and trading-centres, and they founded colonies at Dublin, Wexford, Waterford and Limerick.

From time to time, the Irish struck back and, in 1014, their great leader, Brian Boru, broke the power of the Danes at Clontarf. Brian himself was killed, and as no strong ruler arose, Ireland fell into a state of anarchy for the next century.

Barbaric life: an Irish king, in his bath, shares a meal of horse-flesh with some of his subjects.

Primitive transport: a 13th century picture of two Connaught men crossing a lake in their coracle.

An early Celtic cross. Before the coming of the Vikings, Irish warriors respected churches and monasteries which were therefore filled with rich shrines, altar vessels, books and magnificent metalwork.

Kings and quarrels

For centuries, Ireland was divided up into dozens of little kingdoms, each ruled by its chief or king. These were grouped under overlords who were themselves subject to more powerful kings.

Above them all was the Ard-ri or High King, an empty title which nevertheless caused endless disputes. The chieftains quarrelled and fought continuously but the High King was seldom strong enough to assert his authority and to unite the country. Yet the tribesmen observed a set of laws called the Brehon Laws which went back to the misty days of the Druids.

Irish monasteries

Soon after the coming of Christianity, Findian of Clonard founded the Irish type of monastery, a collection of huts and beehive cells surrounded by a ditch, like a military encampment. The monks devoted them-selves to learning and, in the sixth century, founded monastic schools which were among the most famous in Europe. From these monasteries, Irish missionaries went out to Scotland, Northumbria, France, Italy, Switzerland, Germany and Iceland.

Thus, at the time of the first Viking raids, Ireland possessed rich monasteries filled with priceless books and church ornaments, but the country had no large towns, no stone bridges or paved roads, no coinage or central government.

Easy victims

Chiefs, freemen and slaves lived in wattle huts and thatched halls, and they met at assemblies rather like market fairs. But they never organised themselves into a feudal state ruled by one king and, when the Vikings came and, after them, the Normans, they were easy victims for a ruthless invader.

The ancient kingdoms of Ireland and the English "Pale", a defended area surrounding Dublin, and formed after Henry II became Ireland's overlord.

The Vikings bring trade

The Viking invaders brought benefits as well as disasters. They knew far more about trade and living in towns than the Irish and, from Dublin, Waterford, Wexford and other seaport towns which they founded, a flourishing commerce grew up. Foreign traders—Flemings and Italians—came to settle there and it was through these trading centres that Ireland came into contact with the rest of Europe.

... and some stay

The Vikings intermarried with the Irish, became Christians, influenced Irish art, gave some of their words to the Irish language and taught the Irish to mint coins. But they never settled in Ireland in such large numbers as in England and the country as a whole remained in the hands of the native chieftains.

Effigy of a Norman knight buried at Kilfane, County Kilkenny. In 1169, the first of the Normans sailed to Ireland from Wales where some of them had lost their estates, owing to an upsurge of Welsh power during the wars of Stephen's reign. They were needy adventurers, hoping to recoup their losses by winning lands in Ireland. Their success encouraged Strongbow to follow.

An axe-man splits the skull of his foe. He is probably one of the "galloglasses", mercenaries hired from the Scottish isles by Irish chiefs.

Ireland Betrayed

In 1156, Dermot MacMurrough's enemies drove him from the throne of Leinster. Dermot appealed to Henry II and, given permission to recruit freelances, he went to Richard, Earl of Pembroke ("Strongbow") with the promise of his daughter in marriage and the throne of Leinster. He also enlisted Robert Fitz-Stephen and Maurice Fitz-Gerald, who made up a force of Norman knights and foot-soldiers, crossed to Ireland in 1169 and restored Dermot to his throne.

Next year, Strongbow landed with a much larger force to capture Waterford and Dublin, to marry Dermot's daughter and to dream of making himself High King of Ireland. Henry II had no intention of allowing his barons to set themselves up as independent rulers; he crossed with an army to Ireland, where Strongbow and most of the Irish kings promptly submitted to his authority. He allowed Strongbow to keep Leinster as a fief and the Norman knights to retain their conquests, since they acknowledged him as their overlord. Thus it was, through Irish feuds and Norman greed, that the English first got themselves involved in Ireland.

Bagibun Head, near Wexford, where Strongbow's advance party of 10 knights and 70 archers landed and won an amazing victory over 3,000 Irishmen.

Henry II (above), whose overlordship or Ireland added one more domain to his vast possessions. Henry's attitude to the Irish adventure was both cunning and wary. He was pleased to see some of the discontented Normans leave Wales, for that fitted in with his plans to come to friendly terms with the Welsh leaders. But he was furious when he heard of Strongbow's marriage, and ordered him home. He did not intend to have Normans setting themselves up as independent princes on the borders of his empire.

After Strongbow and the Irish kings had submitted, Henry appointed his own son, John, Lord of Ireland. However, John behaved so insultingly to the Irish that Henry had to bring him home.

Massacre at Waterford

Strongbow decided to go to Ireland because he was down on his luck. A supporter of Stephen in the civil war, he had lost lands, favour and probably his earldom after Henry II came to the throne. By no means certain he had the King's consent, he landed near Waterford with about 1600 troops and laid siege to the city, which was governed by two Danish chiefs.

Repulsed by the defenders, Strongbow's men noticed a house projecting over the walls and supported by props from outside. These were cut and the house fell, making a breach through which the Normans rushed into the streets. They massacred the inhabitants until Dermot himself called an end to the slaughter; then, amid the ruins, Strongbow married Dermot's daughter, Eva.

After this, he captured Dublin but, on Dermot's death, he had such difficulty in trying to hold Leinster that he went to Henry II, asking for help and surrendering all his lands and castles. Henry crossed over and put his own men in charge, Strongbow keeping only Kildare; later, he received Leinster back.

When Strongbow died in 1176, he was buried in the Cathedral Church of Dublin, where his effigy and that of his wife can still be seen (right).

John "Softsword"

Was John really the worst king who ever occupied the English throne, or was he simply unlucky? Certainly, he was cruel, greedy and treacherous, but he had to face Philip Augustus, and Pope Innocent III, two of the greatest figures in the Middle Ages; he was always short of money, his English barons no longer had much interest in the French possessions and his continental vassals were as treacherous as he was.

The trouble with John was failure—he lost Normandy, Anjou, Touraine and Maine; of all the territories of William the Conqueror and Geoffrey of Anjou, only the Channel Islands were left. Men called him "Softsword", though this was not quite fair. At times, John would show military skill equal to his brother, Richard's, though, at others, he would sink into idleness and despair. The truth was he could trust nobody.

Philip encircled Normandy and John had offended so many barons in so many ways that they would not fight. In 1204, Normandy was lost and though John made great plans to win it back, his allies were crushed at Bouvines in 1214. Failure on this scale led straight to Magna Carta and civil war.

A 14th century manuscript shows John and Philip Augustus sealing a truce with the traditional kiss of peace. In Richard I's reign, they had plotted together to share his possessions and neither trusted the other.

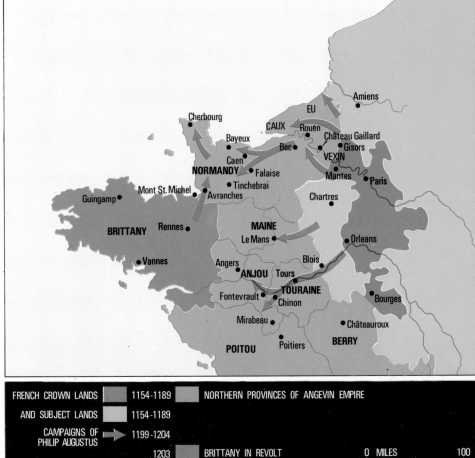

FRENCH CROWN LANDS	1154-1189	NORTHERN PROVINCES OF ANGEVIN EMPIRE
AND SUBJECT LANDS	1154-1189	
CAMPAIGNS OF PHILIP AUGUSTUS	1199-1204	
	1203	BRITTANY IN REVOLT
	1203-1204	CONQUESTS OF REBELS

0 MILES 100
0 KMS. 150

Map of Northern France, showing Philip Augustus's conquest of Normandy and the Angevin possessions. You can see how John's folly caused Normandy to be surrounded by enemies; his marriage roused rebellion in Poitou; the murder of Arthur caused Bretons and Angevins to go over to Philip, and many of the Normans felt no loyalty towards the English King.

The key to Normandy's defence was Chateau Gaillard ("Saucy Castle"), Richard I's masterpiece which he built near the French border. It was supposed to be impregnable, but Philip captured it and when Rouen fell soon afterwards, Normandy was lost.

A rival put to death

Arthur of Brittany was the son of Geoffrey, one of John's older brothers; it could be said, therefore, that he had a better right to the English throne than John. However, John was duly crowned. Meanwhile, young Arthur and his friends had secured Anjou, Touraine and Maine, for which Arthur immediately did homage to Philip Augustus. Nothing suited Philip better than to support Arthur, for he meant thereby to win back all the English lands in France.

However, John recovered his authority until, by marrying the intended bride of a French nobleman, he infuriated the turbulent barons of Poitou. This gave Philip his chance. Summoning Arthur to help, he invaded Normandy, while Arthur laid siege to old Eleanor of Aquitaine in Mirabeau Castle. Eleanor sent word to John who took the besiegers by surprise, rescued his mother and captured Arthur. He imprisoned him, first at Falaise and then at Rouen, in the custody of Hubert de Burgh.

At this time, dangerous rivals were usually done away with and, although we do not know the details, Arthur was put to death. Some said he was blinded and thrown into the river; others declared that John killed him with his own hands.

Arthur pleads for his life with Hubert de Burgh. In fact, Arthur was not a little boy at the time of his capture, but a youth of 16.

John hunting (below): like all medieval monarchs, he enlivened his travels about the country with hunting and enforced the forest laws.

Cruel King John

Cruel, faithless, greedy, lustful and insolent, a man without respect for God, Pope, barons or people—that was how the monkish chroniclers described John. They saw him as a robber of Church property, a king who brought suffering and loss to the clergy, so they painted him in the blackest colours, and we know that some of their accusations were false.

The barons hated John because, by his insults and money-grabbing, he overstepped all the bounds of custom and law. In times of war, a king could ask for *scutage* ("shield money") but John demanded it more often and at twice the old rate. When a baron inherited his estates, he paid a "relief"—about £100—but John demanded thousands; he took huge sums when heiresses married, drained the wealth from minors' estates, imprisoned men without cause, fined them for losing the King's "goodwill", took their sons as hostages, insulted their wives and daughters and filled the land with foreigners hired to carry out his orders. He lost his quarrel with France, the Pope and the barons because no man could love this tyrant or willingly come to his aid.

Pope Innocent III. To assert the Church's authority, he excommunicated 4 kings. At this time, almost all men in Western Europe from the King to the lowliest peasant were members of the Catholic Church, and recognised the Pope as its Supreme Head.

The great seal of John. Despite his faults, John knew how to govern; he attended law-courts, granted charters, minted good coins and built a navy.

John's struggle with the Pope

John's quarrel with the Pope arose over the appointment of the Archbishop of Canterbury. The monks elected their own sub-prior. John told them to choose a friend of his and the Pope set aside both candidates and commanded the monks to elect Stephen Langton, an English Cardinal living abroad. In rage, John declared he would hang Langton if he set foot in the kingdom.

At this, Innocent placed England under an *interdict*, which forbade Church services and burial of the dead. The people were terrified, but John helped himself to Church treasure, and went campaigning in the north, where he defeated William the Lion of Scotland.

After John yielded his kingdom to the Pope, Innocent III sent this Bull (papal command), telling the churchmen, nobles and people of Ireland to remain faithful to John. Innocent's policy was to make the Pope stronger than any king in Europe.

Threat of invasion

The Pope's reply was to excommunicate John and to order Philip Augustus to drive him from the throne. Philip was about to invade, when John, finding no support from his barons or people, offered to surrender England to the Pope.

Innocent accepted and, upon John doing homage, gave him back the kingdom to hold as a papal fief. For the time being, John had outmanoeuvred his enemies and gained a most powerful ally.

The King's huntsman (above) leads the chase.

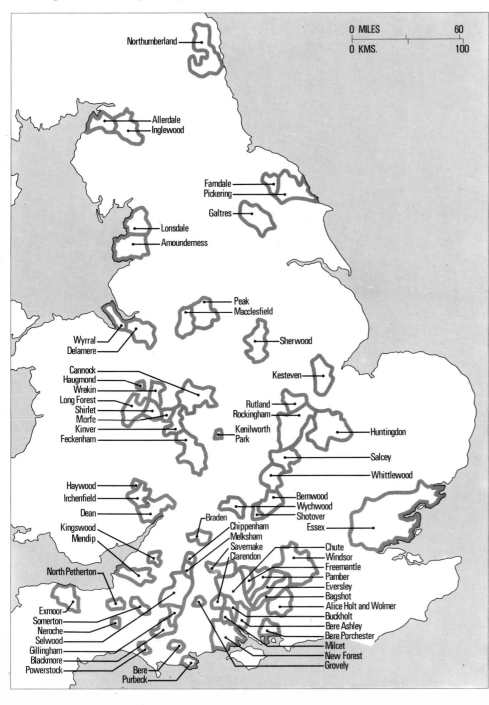

Map labels:
Northumberland
Allerdale
Inglewood
Farndale
Pickering
Galtres
Lonsdale
Amounderness
Peak
Macclesfield
Wyrral
Delamere
Sherwood
Cannock
Haughmond
Wrekin
Long Forest
Shirlet
Morfe
Kinver
Feckenham
Kesteven
Rutland
Rockingham
Kenilworth Park
Huntingdon
Salcey
Whittlewood
Haywood
Irchenfield
Dean
Braden
Bernwood
Wychwood
Shotover
Essex
Chippenham
Melksham
Savernake
Clarendon
Kingswood
Mendip
North Petherton
Chute
Windsor
Freemantle
Pamber
Eversley
Bagshot
Alice Holt and Wolmer
Buckholt
Bere Ashley
Bere Porchester
Milcet
New Forest
Grovely
Exmoor
Somerton
Neroche
Selwood
Gillingham
Blackmore
Powerstock
Bere Purbeck

0 MILES 60
0 KMS. 100

A castle under attack (above) during the civil war between John and the barons.

Hunting—the passion of kings

Medieval kings adored hunting, a passion that was shared by everyone—nobles, abbots, townsmen and peasants. No matter how severe the law, men would hunt whenever they had the chance.

William the Conqueror loved "the tall deer as if he were their father", his sons and Henry II hunted with fanatical zest and by John's reign, royal forests covered a third of the country and included whole counties, such as Essex.

In these areas, the forest laws were severe; no man could hunt deer or wild boars, take timber or clear the undergrowth, carry a bow or keep a dog unless it was "lawed", i.e. had three claws removed from a fore-paw to make it useless for hunting.

All who lived in the forest were subject to strict regulations by the hated foresters, and any offence against the forest laws was punished with savage cruelty. If an offender remained uncaught, whole villages and towns would be fined and John made the utmost use of the forest laws to increase his income.

The map (left) shows the royal forests in the 13th century. Not all the land was densely wooded and many towns and villages lay within the royal forests.

49

The Magna Carta

The barons had dozens of grievances against John. He had lost Normandy and the French possessions, he demanded their services abroad in a new war against Philip Augustus, he expected "aids" and scutages beyond all reason, imposed huge fines and stripped estates in his care. He affronted their dignity and gave favours to foreign ruffians, he trusted no-one and, above all, no-one felt safe, as he prowled about the kingdom, finding excuses to strike down one man, to ruin another.

So they met together to demand the rights granted to their class by Henry I and, with Langton's help, they drew up Magna Carta and forced John to seal it and to swear to keep it. The immediate effect was not peace but civil war that lasted until after John was dead.

Nevertheless, Magna Carta was a landmark. It laid down the idea that the country should be ruled by law and not by the will of a king, and although the barons had had no thought for the common people, the Charter became the banner for those who believed in the rights of an Englishman to freedom and justice.

In November 1214, the barons met at Bury St Edmunds and swore, one by one on the high altar, that if John refused their claims they would make war on him until he agreed to grant their rights by a charter.

Halting civil war

By Spring 1215, many of the barons had taken up arms, had entered London and sent appeals for help to Philip Augustus. John garrisoned his castles but showed himself willing to come to terms by proposing that a court should be convened to arrange peace.

The barons refused, but presently took the advice of a group headed by Stephen Langton, Hubert de Burgh and William Marshal, who helped draw up a charter and arranged a meeting with the King. These three, who were trusted by both sides, did their utmost to avoid civil war.

The King sets his seal

John was at Windsor, the barons at Staines, and when safe conduct had been arranged, both parties met at

Runnymede, the small island in the River Thames, near Windsor, where John met the barons, led by Robert

Fitz-Walter and Eustace de Vesci, Lord of Alnwick, a dubious pair already accused of treachery.

Runnymede on 15th June. The meeting was short and tense; the King set his seal, not on the Charter, but on a draft called the Articles of the Barons. Four days later, when copies had been made to be sent round the country, the Great Seal was finally attached to the Magna Carta.

After Runnymede

John certainly took steps to see that the agreement was carried out, for he ordered all the sheriffs to have the Charter publicly read and to appoint knights in every county to look into grievances and evil customs. However, finding the barons still under arms and apparently un-

willing to trust him, he looked for ways to escape from his promises. In August, a letter arrived from the Pope, condemning the Charter as illegal and, by autumn, John had obtained sufficient mercenary troops from abroad to make war on his opponents.

In a whirlwind campaign, he subdued county after county with such fury that the barons turned once more to Philip Augustus and, in May 1216, a French army, commanded by Philip's son, Louis, landed in Kent. By now, the barons' objective was to overthrow John completely and put the French prince on the throne.

King John at Runnymede. At his elbow, Langton, the Archbishop, urges him to accept the clauses.

Langton tried all along to avoid civil war, but John, once freed from his oath, was bent on revenge.

King John (1199–1216), said to be handsome, well-built and of most charming manners. He was clever and well-read, but totally selfish and untrustworthy.

The Articles of the Barons, the first draft of the Charter, which the barons presented at Runnymede. Instead of bringing peace, it led to savage fighting and the arrival in England of a French army.

Liberties and rights

The Charter contained sixty-three clauses dealing with the Church, baronage, "aids" and scutages, justice, trade and various other points. The famous Clause 29 declared, "No free man is to be taken or imprisoned or deprived of his property or outlawed or molested . . . except by the lawful judgement of his equals or by the law of the land".

In later times, men came to regard Magna Carta as the foundation of their liberties and of their right to trial by jury and to fair taxation. Nothing could be further from the truth. By "liberties", the barons meant their own privileges, especially their rights to hold private courts, and, by "freemen", they meant themselves and their own class, not the common people. Nevertheless, Magna Carta *was* a declaration of rights and justice against tyranny.

The Men who Built

The wealth of medieval society lay principally in the land. It was the peasants' labour that paid for the king's wars, the barons' tournaments and the bishops' palaces. Along with the peasant, the skilled craftsman was essential to the community. Every town, monastery and village had its smiths, masons, carpenters, wheelwrights and armourers. There were also artists, woodcarvers, weavers and potters, all carrying on their trade or "mystery"—how else would the castles, monasteries and cathedrals have been built and decorated?

Industry was looked on as a service to the community and the craft guilds constantly insisted that bad workmanship damaged their members' reputation. Artisans were therefore bidden to carry out their work, not in closed workshops, but in "the sight of the people". Apprenticeship—the training of a boy by a master craftsman—started early in the thirteenth century in London and quickly spread to every town. After seven years spent in learning his trade, the apprentice became a journeyman, working for a daily wage until he could rise to become a master-craftsman.

Artisans in the blacksmith's shop (above). The smith is making a small article, perhaps a bolt or a hinge, while his assistant drills a hole in a metal bar, possibly to strengthen a cart.

Carpenters (left) using a double-handed saw to make planks; their principal tools were hammer, saw, chisels, auger for making holes and adze for smoothing wood (a kind of axe with a curved blade at right angles to the shaft).

Capital letter in a medieval manuscript, showing an apprentice mixing paint for his master who is at work on a mural painting.

An iron miner with his pick, from a church brass. Several monasteries drew incomes from iron mines which they owned; miners received a licence to work iron in a district until the supply was exhausted.

Blacksmith at work on a horseshoe; his assistant keeps the forge fire going with a pair of hand bellows.

Weavers and stone masons

Woollen cloth-making was the most widespread industry and employed the largest number of craftsmen; its importance was marked by royal protection and by the wealth of the weavers' guilds.

Close behind came the building trade, in which the top craftsmen were the stone masons who travelled about the country and were sometimes accommodated in the "masons' lodge"—there was for instance, a "school" of West country masons who built many churches and cathedrals. The master mason was the architect of his day, drawing plans for a new building and taking charge of the entire operation.

Miners

"Free mining" allowed miners to move about—King John gave the tinners a charter—and even to hold their own courts. Coal came from the northern hills and sea-cliffs, iron from the Forest of Dean, lead and silver from Derbyshire, Cumberland and the Mendip Hills, while Cornish and Devon tin supplied most of Europe's needs.

Making things of iron

In his smithy, the blacksmith made almost every metal article required for everyday use, hammering small pieces of semi-molten iron into shape. By the thirteenth century, powerful bellows, driven by water wheels, heated the fire to produce a liquid metal which set hard and brittle. This was pig-iron. Allowed to go cold, broken up and re-heated, it produced steel.

Charcoal was the essential fuel for smelting and working iron, for it produced fiercer heat than coal.

The Men who Sold

Under feudal law, the holder of land could impose his will upon all who lived on his estates, so townsfolk found themselves under the rule of the king's officials or of a baron or of some tyrannical abbot. From an early date, therefore, the leading burgesses tried to win freedom to run the town's affairs by buying a charter of liberties. The Church rarely yielded its rights, but kings and barons, always in need of money, were more willing to grant charters in return for an annual rent—Richard I and John granted scores of charters.

Once free, the burgesses would run the town for their own profit and also for the general good of the people. But there was little goodwill towards outsiders. Each town strove to become self-dependent and usually regarded neighbouring towns with open hostility. The guilds tried to restrict foreign merchants (who often had the king's favour) to wholesale trading, i.e. to bringing in goods, such as spices or silks, but not to selling them to the public. Nevertheless, London, in particular, had its groups of foreign merchants—Flemings, Italians, Gascons and the Hansards from north Germany.

The Jews House in Lincoln. In Henry's reign, Aaron of Lincoln was the richest man in England; he lent vast sums to the King and paid for the building of at least 9 abbeys.

Traders in money

Jews were cruelly treated in the Middle Ages. English kings found them useful because they lent money and could be made to pay heavy fines and "reliefs". Since they were barred from normal trade, Jews had to take to money-lending and kings, nobles, abbots and merchants relied on them for ready cash. Interest rates were high but, at death, all the property of a Jew went to the Exchequer.

Suspicion and hatred were easily stirred up and terrible massacres of Jews took place in Europe and, during Richard I's reign, in England too. Edward I, finding he could borrow from Italian bankers, banished all Jews from the kingdom in 1290.

A thriving town, where merchants and craftsmen display their goods on counters set across the fronts of their houses. They made or prepared their wares in down-stairs workshops and lived upstairs.

Goods from far and wide

Most of the country's trade was carried on in the town market, held on one day a week, and in the annual fairs which lasted a week. The great fairs at Winchester, London and Stourbridge attracted buyers from far and wide; here were sold the country's finest wool and broadcloth, its best hides, herrings, hams, altar vessels and honey, its salt, iron, lead and tin. Italian merchants brought silks, glassware and spices, Flemings came with linen, Spaniards with iron, Gascons with wine and Easterlings with furs, tar, tallow and amber.

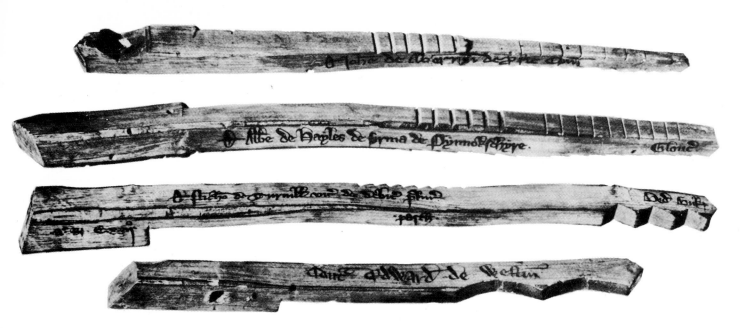

13th century tally sticks which were used as receipts. Notches were cut to show the amount of a payment—big notches for pounds, smaller ones for shillings and the smallest for pence. The stick was then split and the longer piece was kept by the payer. When accounts were checked, the two pieces would "tally".

Henry II's charter to the London weavers, granting them their guild. Craft guilds existed in 100 English towns and there were 80 guilds in London. Each guild, under its warden, was open only to skilled craftsmen.

Seal of the Corporation of Shrewsbury of about 1425. Shrewsbury has over 30 charters, the first being granted by Henry I.

The towns' rights

The foremost privileges which townsfolk obtained when they bought a charter were the rights to collect the town dues, to hold their own court, elect their own magistrates, mayor and bailiffs, to form a "guild merchant" and to hold a market.

The guilds

The first "guild merchant" was formed in Burford in 1087; these early guilds were associations of all the traders in a town. From the twelfth century, craftsmen formed separate craft guilds for masters, journeymen and apprentices. The guilds fixed wages and prices, punished cheats and helped members who were sick, and their widows and orphans.

The Extravagant Monarch-Henry III

When, as a boy of nine, Henry III came to the throne, the royalists rallied to protect him. King John was dead, and no-one could pretend that his little son was a tyrant, not even the barons who had offered the crown to Louis of France. The French were driven out and the kingdom was well governed, first by William Marshal, the aged Earl of Pembroke, and then by Hubert de Burgh.

However, this situation could not last. At twenty, Henry took over the reins of government and showed that he had less aptitude for kingship than his father. He was not wicked, but weak. In his piety, he allowed the Pope to extract enormous sums of money from the country; in his dislike of English advisers, he surrounded himself with greedy foreigners and, in his generosity, he loaded his friends with princely gifts. None of these faults would have harmed him if he had been successful, but extravagance at home was followed by military failure abroad. When the kingdom was almost bankrupt, the barons demanded a say in the government, insisting that Henry should rule with the aid of a council. The result was a civil war.

Henry's seal; at heart Henry was a decent man, devout, affectionate and fond of beautiful things. As a ruler, he was lacking in judgment, yet he left the kingdom better than he found it.

A young king's protectors

As soon as young Henry was crowned, a royalist party, headed by William Marshal, Ranulf of Chester, Peter des Roches and Hubert de Burgh, set about ridding the country of the French mercenaries whom the Dauphin Louis had brought with him when he came to take John's crown. After the Frenchmen had been defeated, the royalists turned their attention to regaining all the King's castles and driving out the lawless foreigners whom John had rewarded with titles and estates.

To win public support and to demonstrate the government's good intentions, Marshal issued a new

Henry III was crowned twice; at Gloucester in 1216, when the only crown available was his mother's gold circlet, and at Westminster in 1221. Later, Henry re-built Edward the Confessor's church at Westminster.

edition of Magna Carta and also a Charter of the Forests. He died in 1219, after a career of unswerving loyalty to the Crown, and, for the next thirteen years, the country was practically ruled by Hubert de Burgh, the Justiciar. While Peter des Roches took charge of the young King's upbringing, management of Church affairs was in the hands of Stephen Langton, the wise Archbishop of Canterbury.

The Pope, however, did not cease taking a close interest in the kingdom which John had surrendered to him, and the papal legates exercised a good deal of influence. When he grew up, the devout King Henry never forgot that the Pope was his overlord; he accepted his authority without question and obediently parted with huge sums of money to help support the papal finances.

A miserable failure

For much of his reign, Henry cherished hopes of recovering Normandy and the rest of the lands in France which his father had lost. At different times, he fitted out three impressive expeditions and himself took part in some fighting, but he failed miserably, partly through treacherous allies, but mostly through his complete lack of military skill.

In 1232, now twenty-five, he dismissed de Burgh and announced that he would rule the country; influenced by Peter des Roches, from Poitou, Henry replaced his English officials with Bretons and Poitevins on whom he lavished

Louis VIII of France (left); as a prince, he fought in England and, later, his policy was to stop Henry winning back the Angevin lands.

titles and estates. These foreign favourites angered the English nobles and the position became worse when Henry married Eleanor of Provence, who brought with her a horde of hard-up relations whom Henry rewarded with more gifts, bishoprics and heiresses. Nor were they all. Henry's mother, Isabella of Angoulême, had re-married in Poitou and had a second family; after Henry's disastrous French expedition of 1242, Isabella's children came trooping into England to enjoy the bounty of their royal half-brother.

Henry's hopes in France were ended by the Treaty of Paris, 1259, when he and Louis IX agreed that Normandy, Anjou, Maine and Poitou should be French, while the English King kept Gascony, formerly called Aquitaine.

The 16th century artist who drew this picture did not realise that cannons had not been invented in Henry III's reign! The drawing shows the final defeat of Louis' invasion force.

In 1217, Henry's supporters were outnumbered by the rebel barons and the French army, which held London and most of the south.

The French were defeated at Lincoln, and Louis took refuge in London where the citizens were strongly on his side.

Meanwhile, his wife collected an army which embarked in 80 vessels, but, off Sandwich, this fleet was intercepted by a smaller force commanded by de Burgh. Sailing to windward, he ordered his sailors to throw lime at the enemy; the wind carried it into their faces and caused such confusion that the French were completely routed and all Louis' hopes came to an end.

A New Age

The reign of Henry III lasted for fifty-six years and spanned a period of tremendous mental and spiritual advance. Universities came into existence in England, France and Italy; the works of Aristotle and other philosophers, which had passed from Greek into Arabic and thence into Latin, caused men to ask questions and to look for answers in nature and the outside world. Science was re-born when men like Grosseteste and Roger Bacon not only wrote about astronomy, physics and mathematics, but actually carried out experiments. The monasteries no longer held all the secrets of knowledge; England produced some remarkable churchmen and scholars, and the friars came out in the world preaching and teaching.

Henry III's love of splendour was expressed in buildings, notably the new Abbey of Westminster. The massive Norman style of architecture gave way to a lighter, more gracious style, with pointed arches and wide multiple windows. Glass came into use, castles reached perfection, houses began to be made of brick, and fireplaces and chimneys made their appearance. In many ways, the thirteenth century was a new age.

Pope Gregory IX, from a mosaic in the Vatican. In 1237, when Henry III was in trouble with the barons, he sent his own representative (a papal legate) to help and advise him.

Henry III in Westminster Abbey (opposite page): a superb example of the new lifelike sculpture.

Building Solomon's temple: a manuscript drawing shows that medieval builders knew how to use a pulley.

French architect's sketch of buttresses. By taking the weight and thrust of the roof, they allowed Gothic cathedrals to have thin walls and huge windows.

Art and science flourish

One of the most exciting revolutions in art was the emergence of Gothic architecture. Pointed arches, slender columns, larger windows produced buildings of astonishing beauty. Salisbury and Lincoln cathedrals are masterpieces, so are the west fronts at Wells and Peterborough. These and many cathedral alterations are typically English, but Westminster Abbey is French in design. Henry's court was a centre for artists and craftsmen and he imported French masons and sculptors. English craftsmen made exquisite floor-tiles, carvings and wrought-iron work for churches.

Meanwhile, at Oxford, Grosseteste and Bacon were tackling problems in science by observation and experiment. They studied heat and light, made telescopes and gunpowder; Bacon envisaged flying-machines and horseless chariots.

The Rivalry for Power

Because Henry III came to the throne as a child, the government had to be taken into the hands of a small group of powerful ministers. For a number of years, this system worked well, chiefly because William Marshal, Stephen Langton and Hubert de Burgh were men of remarkable ability and loyalty. Nevertheless, much of Henry's later troubles arose from the resentment which he felt towards these strong paternal protectors. Hence, he was glad to be rid of Hubert de Burgh, who received no thanks for his long and devoted service, and to show favour to his friends from France.

The English nobles found a leader in Richard Marshal, who informed Henry that if he did not dismiss Peter des Roches and the others, the barons would elect a new king. However, Richard died, and it was among the foreigners that the barons found their next leader in Simon de Montfort. The King was brought to heel and the foreigners were expelled. Yet, in the end, Henry won through all his troubles; de Montfort was slain, the King's son triumphed everywhere and the old King ended his days in a land both peaceful and prosperous.

A mounted knight of the early 13th century. Armed like one of Richard I's crusaders, his suit of mail extends to gloves covering the hands, and his flat-topped helm completely covers the head and face. Knights were now wearing a loose linen garment, called a "gown", over the hauberk. Partial horse-armour had now been introduced, and notice the high saddle-bow which protects the rider's stomach. By Henry III's Assize of Arms 1242, men with an income of £15 a year were to serve on horseback; those with £2–£5 were to carry bows.

The Archbishop of Canterbury and the Archbishop of London, two of the churchmen who wielded immense power in England. As educated men, constantly travelling about the continent and, as great landowners, they had much influence in public affairs. Many bishops were anything but godly men, for kings rewarded their servants by getting them made bishops.

In Henry's reign, the Pope rewarded French and Italian clergy by giving them English "livings" or benefices, as Church positions were called.

White Castle, Monmouthshire (built 1220–1240), one of the properties which de Burgh acquired while serving the King.

A popular hero

Hubert de Burgh served John as Chamberlain, as Prince Arthur's keeper, as sheriff, soldier and, finally, as Justiciar. The defender of Dover Castle and victor of the sea-battle off Sandwich became a popular hero and, after William Marshal's death, ruler of the country.

He acted almost always in the best interests of England and young Henry, but, in climbing, he had enriched himself and made many enemies. Henry, offended because de Burgh opposed his wild schemes for foreign conquest, suddenly dismissed the Justiciar and imprisoned him. Before his death in 1234, he was pardoned and restored to his earldom.

Hubert (below) about to be dragged from the chapel in which he took sanctuary after his downfall.

Simon de Montfort

The traditional view of Simon de Montfort is of the foreigner who became champion of the Englishman's liberties, founder of Parliament and hero of the common people. The facts of his career do not fit this glowing legend. De Montfort came to England as a young man and quickly won Henry III's favour; gifted and charming, he obtained the earldom of Leicester, married the King's sister, held high office and, by his arrogance, earned the enmity of the great barons.

When Henry found new favourites, de Montfort joined the barons in demanding reform and helped to compel the King to accept the Provisions of Oxford, whereby a council of magnates would govern the country. Henry's breaking of the agreement led to the battle of Lewes, where de Montfort captured the King and took his son Edward hostage. Now ruler of the country, he called the famous Parliament of 1265, packed with his supporters. But his power had no solid foundation. Already, his arrogance had alarmed the nobles and when Prince Edward escaped, de Montfort was doomed. He died in battle at Evesham, just fifteen months after the victory at Lewes.

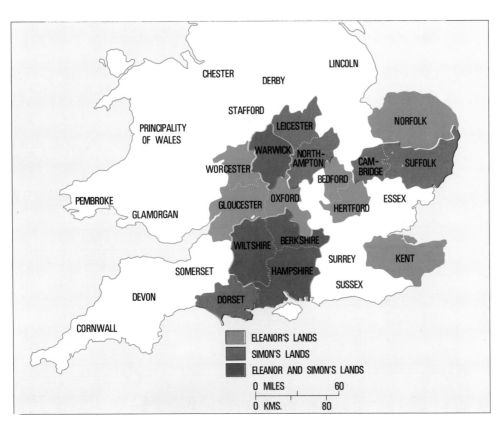

A great landowner

As this map shows, Simon de Montfort became the greatest landowner in the realm when he married the King's sister, Eleanor. Henry III had already granted him the earldom of Leicester, so the marriage gave him control of the centre of England, East Anglia and the important county of Kent.

As long as he stood high in the King's favour, the jealousy of other nobles could not prevent Simon from taking a leading place in Court; however, he began to treat Henry in a truculent manner when he found that his brother-in-law was mean about money and would not provide the income which he looked upon as his right.

This grievance and the fact that on his return from four years' service as Governor of Gascony, he felt himself excluded from the inner circle of the King's advisers, seem to have decided him to take the lead in the barons' rebellion against Henry's misgovernment.

Kenilworth Castle, Simon de Montfort's family seat where Prince Edward was held captive. He afterwards defeated Simon's son outside the castle.

In the background, you can see the 12th century keep, the oldest part of the castle which, in later years, was much damaged by Cromwell's soldiers. In its hey-day, Kenilworth was an almost impregnable fortress, being protected by a wide lake. Henry III gave it to his sister, the wife of de Montfort, and, after Evesham, Young Simon held it against a long siege until forced to surrender by hunger.

The King is captured

When Henry III refused to accept government by a council of barons, both sides took up arms. The King's forces were led by his son, "the Lord Edward", and barons' by Simon de Montfort.

They met at Lewes on May 14th 1264. Prince Edward charged de Montfort's Londoners so furiously that he drove them from the field and pursued them across country. But while he was cutting them down, Simon's other troops routed the royalists and captured the King, so that, when Edward returned, the battle was over.

He took refuge in a friary but, on the following day he was made a hostage to make sure that the terms would be carried out, and he went into captivity for a year, spent mostly at Kenilworth Castle.

First round to the barons: a manuscript picture shows Henry III captured by de Montfort at the Battle of Lewes. The King, though he lacked military skill, commanded the centre of his army, escaped from the field and was captured in Lewes Priory.

The emblem of Simon de Montfort, son of the celebrated French crusader. The shield with its silver fork-tailed lion is in Westminster Abbey.

After the battle of Evesham, Earl Simon's body is cut to pieces. His head was sent as a souvenir to the wife of

Roger Mortimer, Lord of Wigmore, one of the Marcher barons, who hated De Montfort and his ally, Llewelyn.

Second round to the King: Henry III is seen finishing off de Montfort at the Battle of Evesham, 1265. In fact, Prince Edward won the victory and Henry, who had been de Montfort's captive, had to be rescued from the slaughter.

The royalists recover

After he had captured the King, de Montfort called the Parliament of 1265 but did little to prevent the royalists from recovering.

The first sign in the break-up of his own party came when his strongest ally, Gilbert, Earl of Gloucester, withdrew to the Welsh Marches to join forces with the King's friends. He had, it seems, come to hate Simon's sons and to resent their father's leadership.

Prince Edward was in the custody of Gloucester's brother and it was therefore easy to arrange his escape. Edward immediately rode to join Gloucester at Ludlow where a powerful army gathered round them. Earl Simon was in the West Country with the captured King, but instead of making for London,

he turned for help to his friend, Llewelyn of Wales, and ordered his son Simon to come to their aid. Young Simon marched to Kenilworth where Prince Edward surprised him and captured most of his knights.

The King is saved

Meanwhile, de Montfort halted at Evesham, for the King was tired and the soldiers were hungry. There, on 4th August 1265, Prince Edward attacked, closing in on the Earl and his knights as they stood at bay round the King. Most were killed and Henry himself only escaped by crying, "Slay me not! I am Henry of Winchester!" De Montfort's head was hacked off, but the monks of Evesham buried his body and, in later years, miracles were said to have been wrought at his tomb.

The First Parliament

De Montfort's Parliament of 1265 was by no means the first to be held, nor the first to include elected representatives. It was, however, the first to include *both* the classes which made up the future House of Commons—knights from the shires and burgesses from the towns. Parliament's beginnings go back to the Witan which became the Great Council, a gathering of nobles and bishops who "parleyed" with the king about important matters, especially laws and taxes. "Parliament" also referred to sessions of the king with his principal servants who dealt with justice and administration, and met two or three times a year for this purpose.

By the Provisions of Oxford (1265), the barons demanded three meetings a year "to discuss the common business of the Kingdom", but, by Edward I's reign, parliaments were back under the king's control. Nevertheless, he needed the support of the great barons and churchmen and, from time to time, he also called knights and burgesses. They had no assured place in Parliament, but as sheriffs, tax-collectors and local leaders, they were becoming essential to the government.

The earliest surviving writ and return for a medieval Parliament—the version sent to Buckinghamshire and Bedfordshire, summoning their representatives to the Easter Parliament of 1275 in Edward I's reign.

The King calls Parliament

In Magna Carta, the king agreed that "for obtaining the common council of the kingdom, we will cause to be summoned the archbishops, bishops and greater barons, by our letters under seal; and we will moreover cause to be summoned generally, through our sheriffs, all other who hold of us in chief."

This meant that the king promised to summon all his great lords by name and to tell the sheriffs to have members elected in shires and boroughs—a distinction between Lords and Commons. Henry II had already summoned "one manor" knights to attend the Great Council and, before Magna Carta was sealed, John had called four knights from each shire and had summoned the reeve and four men from each township. This representation of towns was not repeated until De Montfort's parliament.

So far, there was no division into two "Houses" and Parliament tended to meet when and where it suited the king's convenience. Edward I brought his laws before the Great Council, to which he added knights and burgesses as he thought fit. His laws were not debated and "passed", as they would be nowadays. The king explained his proposals, invited Parliament to discuss them and then gave his decision.

Henry III seated above the Charter of 1225 (left), the final version of Magna Carta. Issued and re-issued, it gained new meanings in men's minds.

Who sat in Parliament?

In the thirteenth century, Parliaments were called more frequently, though there was no fixed membership. The nobles and bishops took it for granted that they should advise the king and, in 1265, when de Montfort invited only 5 earls and 18 barons, he made up the numbers with burgesses from certain towns and knights. These were the up-and-coming men, next in wealth and importance to the nobility.

For his part, Edward I summoned the kind of parliament he wanted; sometimes he called "the commons" and the lower clergy, sometimes not. But it never crossed anyone's mind to consult the workers, the 2 million peasants out of a population of $2\frac{1}{2}$ millions. They had to wait 600 years to have a say in how the country was governed.

The Baron: summoned to Parliament by name, he regarded himself as one of the king's "natural" counsellors.

Clergy: bishops, abbots and leading priors attended Parliament, but the clergy in general did not attend regularly.

The Knight: on a writ sent to the sheriff, two knights from each shire were elected by freeholders.

The Burgess: writs were sent to cities and some boroughs for freeholders to elect their representative, usually a rich merchant.

The Peasant: the lowly worker who tilled the farmlands. His life was ruled by the customs of the manor and he had no voice in Parliament, nor did he expect to have a say in matters beyond his understanding.

Parliament Restrains the King

It was in Henry III's reign that the Great Council or Parliament took steps to restrain the King. This arose from his neglect of his traditional advisers for foreign favourites, but the lords insisted upon their ancient right to be consulted about "the common business of the kingdom". No general tax could be levied without their consent and they wanted the money to be wisely spent. So they refused Henry's request for a tax on the grounds that he had not told them how he had spent the previous grant.

In the last seven years of the King's life, there were 16 or 17 parliaments, and they continued to assemble more or less regularly in Edward I's reign. The difference now was that Edward was master of the realm, though he realised that he could govern better and raise taxes if he had the consent and help of the kingdom's leading men. When they felt they had just grievances, they dared to refuse to pay a special tax until Edward had re-confirmed Magna Carta and the Charters of the Forest. Thus was established Parliament's right to have a voice in how the country was governed and taxed.

Charter or Patent Rolls on which the King's grants of land were recorded. Parchment was made from skins of kids and calves, soaked in lime, scraped, stretched and rubbed smooth. Paper did not reach England until the 14th century.

Parchment rolls

In the thirteenth century, the Exchequer kept its accounts on parchment rolls, each the length and breadth of a man, and also on hazelwood tally-sticks. The Chancery's records of the business of the King's household—the charter rolls, patent (public) rolls and so on— were many yards long. Though the monks had long been used to sewing the sections of their books together and enclosing them in wooden covers, parchment rolls were preferred for writs and day-to-day accounts, possibly because the information could be clearly seen on a single sheet.

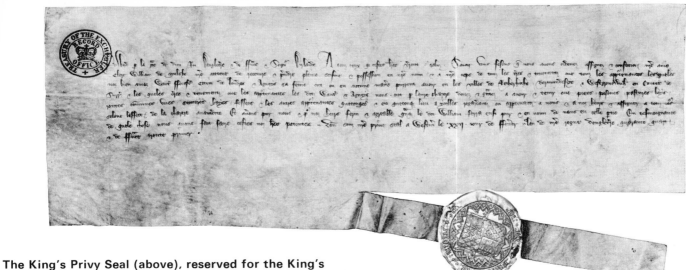

The King's Privy Seal (above), reserved for the King's personal use, dated from King John's reign and was used on documents connected with the King's chamber, with household matters, appointments and privileges. The seal proved that a document was genuine and it was also the authority to obtain money from the Exchequer. In general, it was attached to documents not sufficiently important to require the Great Seal.

Edward I's Parliament of 1274 (below). To his left and right are Alexander III of Scotland and Llywelyn of Wales, and the Archbishops of Canterbury and York. The Chancellor and judges sit on woolsacks in the middle.

Finding Enough Food

Thirteenth century townsmen and villagers lived on food they grew locally, importing practically nothing from other areas, except salt and a few luxuries for the lord. On the demesne and the villagers' strips in the common fields the all-important crops were wheat, barley, rye, oats, peas and beans.

Yields were poor, for little was known about manuring, except that the lord took what manure there was. Meat was fairly plentiful, for the lord owned many animals and the peasants kept pigs and hens, with perhaps an ox, a cow and a few sheep. Despite the law, people trapped birds, rabbits and game. Lack of winter feed meant that most of the cattle had to be killed in autumn and the meat salted or pickled.

In their gardens, the peasants grew vegetables and most had one or two fruit trees. Vast quantities of ale were brewed, with a certain amount of cider, perry and metheglin (a kind of mead); the monasteries produced a good deal of wine, mostly white. There were periods of scarcity but foreigners noticed that Englishmen of all classes ate more and better than their fellows on the continent.

Threshing with a flail, two sticks joined by a leather hinge, to separate the ears of corn from the chaff.

A town worker, using pestle and mortar to pound corn to make starch. This would be used to stiffen the fashionable tall head-dresses.

Hunting in the forest: the king and his nobles killed for sport, the peasant for food. Repressed by laws protecting wild life, the peasants nevertheless missed no opportunity to take game, particularly rabbits and pheasants. Occasionally they killed a deer and cut it up secretly; they all hated the foresters who kept watch against poachers.

The peasants

The majority of peasants had only a few strips in the common fields, with a share in the hay-meadow, the right to graze a cow and to run pigs in the common herd in the charge of the village swineherd.

There emerged a class of better-off peasants who acquired holdings of 40 or 60 strips and paid rent to the lord to avoid compulsory work on his land. Men of this type would clear waste land called "an assart" and farm it in return for a rent.

The poorest villagers, holding few strips or none at all (the "cottars"), lived a hand-to-mouth existence; they were permitted to glean the fields after harvest, the priest would give them alms and the lady of the manor sent them "broken meats" from the lord's table. It was the poor who suffered most in times of drought and "murrain" (cattle plague), though all peasants knew the pinch of hunger at the end of winter when food stocks were exhausted.

Ordinary folk lived on "black bread" made from rye, barley or bean flour, milk, cheese, eggs and an occasional fowl or piece of bacon. Other meats were luxuries, enjoyed at times of "boon work" for the lord and at Yuletide. The manor servants lived better, eating beef, wheat and rye bread, cheese, eggs and an occasional goose.

Top: scene in a bakery where two assistants prepare dough for the baker to put in the oven. In villages, bread was baked at home or in the manorial oven, but in towns, people bought from the bakers. Quality and weight of loaves were strictly controlled and dishonest bakers were often to be seen in the stocks.

Above: a slaughter-house: a pig's gut is cleaned out and the contents burnt, while a pig is slaughtered next door.

A King they Feared- Edward I

Edward I can be called the first English king of England. Certainly, he spoke French, like all the nobility, and he ruled Gascony, a province of France, but he was born and bred in England and his friends and interests were all English. Handsome, with a kingly bearing, Edward was a masterly general who subdued Wales and added it to his kingdom and had almost completed the conquest of Scotland when he died.

However, his real greatness was as a ruler of his people. Known as "the Law-Giver", he suppressed many of the barons' private courts in which it was hard for a man to get true justice, he checked the Church's acquisition of vast amounts of land and he rooted out dishonest sheriffs and judges. Though, towards the end of his reign, when desperate for money, he seized merchants' wool stocks, Edward encouraged the growing wool trade and, in contrast to his father, kept the barons in order. They obeyed, respected and even feared him. In his day, Edward was honoured for a pious act which we would regard as a piece of cruel persecution; in 1290, he expelled all Jews from the kingdom.

In his determination to have order and obedience in all his domains, Edward travelled ceaselessly from Scotland to southern France. Here are some of his ships which have brought him back from Gascony.

In Guienne, the northern part of Gascony, he reduced the power of the barons by encouraging the wine trade with England and by founding new towns. A quarrel between Gascons and French caused Philip the Fair of France to invade Gascony and seize some of Edward's castles. In the war which followed, Edward was hampered by shortage of money and unrest in Scotland; in addition, many of his barons were unwilling to serve abroad. However, he recovered the whole of Gascony and sealed the peace by marrying Philip's sister.

Edward fights the Scots

In 1286, Scotland had no king, but thirteen claimants to the throne. To avoid civil war, the Scots asked Edward, famed as an international expert on law, to judge the case. He decided in favour of John Balliol but insisted upon his own overlordship of Scotland. The Scots resented a king who was no more than Edward's puppet and, taking advantage of the quarrel with France, allied themselves to the French.

In anger, Edward marched north, sacked Berwick and defeated the Scots at Dunbar. Balliol surrendered the throne and Edward retired, leaving his officials in charge. But the Scots proved obstinate. Nothing would reconcile them to English rule and they rallied, first to Wallace and then to Bruce, in order to win their freedom.

The Coronation Chair at Westminster (above), holding the Stone of Scone, sacred to the Scots. Edward removed it in 1296.

Edward I in court dress (right): he was considered to have all the virtues of a true knight.

Edward's Two Beautiful Wives

Until very recent times, in the world of kings, princes and nobles, marriage was a business arrangement. The heads of great families and the advisers of the kings arranged marriages to cement treaties and to unite vast estates; the terms were fiercely argued, especially the amount of the bride's dowry which might include castles, manors and whole provinces. The wishes of the bride and bridegroom troubled no-one. A child of five would be betrothed to a man as old as her father; a prince not yet knighted would find himself promised to a rich widow whom he had never seen.

Edward I was no exception to this heartless rule. When he was fourteen, his father, Henry III, made a treaty with Alfonso of Castile to safeguard Gascony; the boy was sent to Spain where he married Alfonso's sister, Eleanor. She was eight years old. Yet the marriage turned out to be blissfully happy and when Eleanor died, Edward was heartbroken. Nevertheless, a few years later, in order to seal a treaty with France, he married the French King's sister and betrothed his son aged fifteen to the King's five-year-old daughter.

An illuminated capital letter, showing Edward and his wife, Eleanor of Castile; they had 13 children, of whom 5 daughters and a son survived.

The poisoned dagger

After Prince Edward had defeated his father's enemies, he felt able to go on a Crusade to the Holy Land. Eleanor insisted on accompanying him and they reached Acre in 1271. Edward captured Nazareth and then returned to Acre where a messenger arrived from the Emir of Jaffa, and treacherously stabbed him with a poisoned dagger. Edward killed the assassin and Eleanor is said to have saved her husband's life by sucking the poison from his wound.

"Eleanor Crosses"

Soon afterwards, Edward became King and, during the next eighteen years, he and his wife were devoted to each other. In 1290, he was in

Edward I and his first wife, Eleanor. These statues, on an exterior wall of Lincoln Cathedral, show the King wearing his hair longer than his wife's!

Scotland when he learned that his wife was ill with fever; he hurried south and was with her when she died. Her body was taken in solemn procession from Lincolnshire to London and, at every place where a halt was made for the night, Edward ordered an "Eleanor Cross" to be erected. The finest can still be seen at Waltham Cross in Hertfordshire and the last one was raised in the village of Charing, now in the heart of London. The Queen was buried at Westminster Abbey where a splendid tomb was erected in her honour.

The hammer of the Scots

Edward's marriage to Margaret of France was one move in the tactical game that he was forced to play in the closing years of his reign. The girl was beautiful but, more important, she was Philip IV's sister, and the marriage made Gascony safe and ended the war.

Edward could not fight France and the Scots at the same time, for his barons refused to serve abroad and were complaining about the burdens laid upon them. So, in an unforgiving mood, the King turned his attention to Scotland.

John Balliol and the Scottish nobles had knelt to him in homage, and when they defied the authority of their overlord, he had removed Balliol and taken the kingdom into his own keeping. But, taking advantage of his preoccupation in France, the Scots had rebelled and, under the leadership of an insignificant knight, had laid waste the country-side. Edward put down Wallace's rebellion but no sooner was his back turned, than others took Wallace's place.

Exasperated by disobedience and treachery, Edward resolved to suppress the revolt with pitiless severity. The rebels received no mercy and Wallace was put to a cruel death, but, though he hammered them, the Scots did not break. Edward's chief ambition in life brought him failure.

Edward I's second wife, the beautiful Margaret of France, whom he married in 1299 at Canterbury. She was only 17 and the King was nearly 60. They had two sons, Thomas of Norfolk and Edmund Woodstock.

A Kingdom's Defence

The great castles of Britain, which reached perfection in Edward I's reign, had their beginnings in the motte-and-bailey fortresses which William the Conqueror erected. Timber was soon replaced by stone and, by Henry II's reign, the castle's strongest point was the *donjon* or Great Tower, known later as the keep. Because these towers were almost indestructible, many have survived, like the one below at Dover.

But the *donjon* soon went out of fashion, for it had serious disadvantages. The tower was uncomfortable to live in and, in practice, it proved difficult to dislodge an enemy attacking the corners of the base with battering-rams and mines. So, new castles, like Framlingham (right) were designed without the *donjon* but with many towers linked by a curtain-wall that enclosed a courtyard (the ward or bailey) where hall, kitchen, chapel and storerooms could be built. Further refinements were added, such as a vast gatehouse to protect the entrance, an outer defence-work called the barbican and, in concentric castles, an outer ring of walls, lower in height, so that defenders could fire over their comrades' heads.

Framlingham Castle from inside the courtyard: notice the well-top by the tree and the wall-walk once protected by battlements.

Caerphilly Castle in the Welsh Marches: the largest castle in Britain.

Life in a castle

A castle was a home, a fortress, the centre of local government, a prison and, often, a hotel for noble visitors. Its owner, who visited his various estates in turn, would live there for part of the year with his family, servants, priests, soldiers and workmen—the masons and the carpenters who maintained the structure. Royal castles were occupied by the castellan and a permanent garrison.

Life was draughty but not entirely comfortless, for these grim fortresses often contained splendid living-quarters erected in the courtyard, with banqueting-hall, kitchens, gaily-decorated solars, hooded fire-places, sleeping-chambers and toilets.

A big castle would have its own bakery, buttery (wine and ale store), granary, sometimes a piped water-supply and usually a prison-tower or dungeon. The constable often occupied rooms in the gatehouse where he could hold out if his mercenaries turned mutinous.

The square keep of Dover Castle with its crenellated battlements.

Framlingham Castle from the air: built in 1190 by a baron named Roger Bigod, it has no keep, but thirteen flanking towers and a dry moat. The ruin to the left was the Prison Tower.

Arrow-slits in a castle wall: the crossbow was the usual weapon of defence; cumbersome but powerful, it fired a heavy bolt or quarrel. The archer's assistant held a spare bow ready.

Who held the castles?

A castle was the home of a lord. It protected his lands and was the visible proof of his great position in the world. Many of the castles belonged to the king who appointed a castellan or constable to hold each one for him, with a small peacetime garrison, made up to fighting strength in times of emergency by local tenants who held their lands on condition that they did castle-guard when needed.

No baron could build a castle without royal permission and the king could, and often did, confiscate an over-mighty baron's castle.

Strong kings kept a close check on castle-building and permitted it chiefly in areas like the Welsh Marches and along the Scottish border where barons held estates on condition that they maintained law and order in those turbulent districts.

Defence

No army could afford to advance in hostile territory while castles remained untaken in its rear; so, much of medieval warfare consisted of attacking and defending these strongholds.

Defenders, with ample stores of food, relied on the strength of the castle's complicated defences; usually, they sat tight, picked off the enemy with crossbow fire, hurled stones and quicklime on those at the base of the wall and, sometimes,

The colossal gatehouse of Caerphilly Castle which, as though not powerful enough, is guarded by two outer towers. By piling defence on defence, the castle's weakest point, its entrance, was made into the strongest. It was protected, first by the barbican, the moat and the drawbridge; after these was a passage covered by arrow-slits, barred by iron-studded doors and a portcullis. Above the passage were murder-holes through which missiles and liquids could be poured.

made a counter-attack from a side-gate or sally-port. But, ultimately, they had to hope for relief from an ally who could drive the besiegers away.

Attack

The attackers adopted various tactics; having surrounded the castle to cut off all supplies, they would fill in part of the moat to enable ladders and siege-towers to be brought up; siege-engines would hurl bolts and stones at the walls, while sappers dug a tunnel to undermine the corner of a tower.

Most surrenders, however, were brought about by treachery from within, by starvation or, as happened at Caerphilly, by offering honourable terms to the defenders.

A Master-Mason

Having defeated the Welsh, Edward I decided to make further rebellion impossible by building a chain of castles to dominate North Wales. In Master James of St George, a master-mason who had learned his craft in France, he found an architect of genius and, between them, they erected the finest series of medieval fortifications in Europe. An army of workers was assembled and construction went forward at incredible speed. They began with two castles, Flint and Rhuddlan, to command the route from Chester.

Next came Harlech, on the west coast, notable for its colossal gatehouse, a castle in itself. On the north coast, on two long,

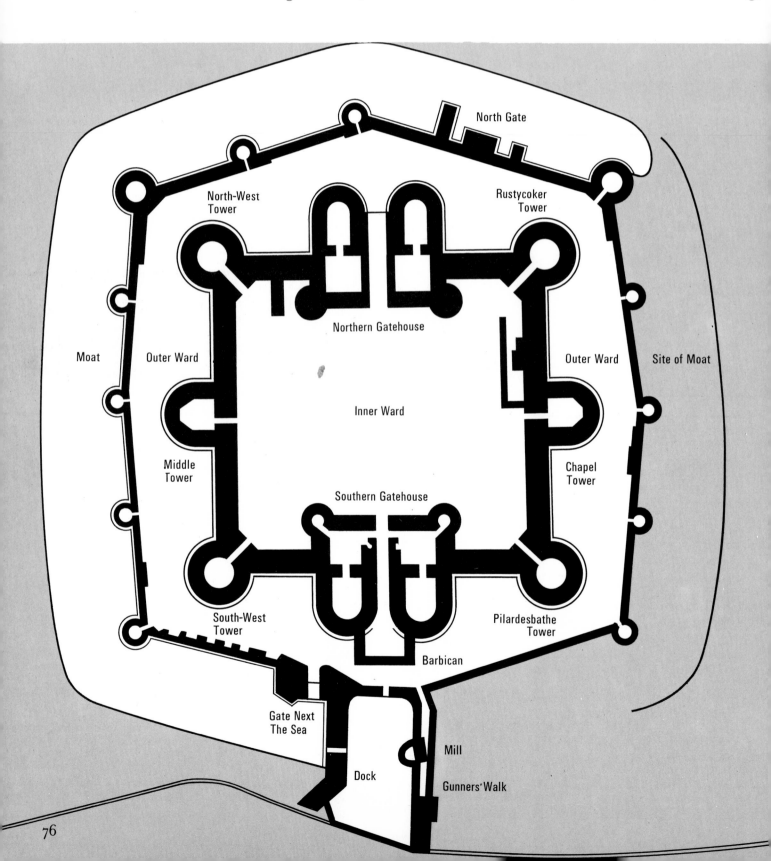

North Gate

North-West Tower

Rustycoker Tower

Northern Gatehouse

Moat

Outer Ward

Outer Ward

Site of Moat

Inner Ward

Middle Tower

Chapel Tower

Southern Gatehouse

South-West Tower

Pilardesbathe Tower

Barbican

Gate Next The Sea

Mill

Dock

Gunners' Walk

narrow sites, Master James built the castles of Caernarvon and Conway, fortresses with walls of tremendous strength, with taller towers, massive gatehouses and wall-passages that enabled the garrisons to move speedily to any threatened point in order to fight off the attackers.

The last of the great strongholds was Beaumaris, the masterpiece whose plan and ruins are shown below. It was never finished but, in design, it remains the perfect concentric castle, with defence overlapping defence, so that, barring treachery, it must have been impregnable until cannon became sufficiently powerful to bring castle warfare to an end.

On the plan, you can see that Beaumaris Castle is symmetrical, that is to say, a tower or gateway on one side is matched by an identical tower or gateway on the other. The aerial view shows the concentric design—an inner ward guarded by high walls and towers is surrounded by an outer ward with a lower wall and small towers. Arrow-fire could thus be directed at an attacker from at least two levels. The barbican in front of the gatehouse protected the dock provided for supply ships. The gatehouses were never finished, for Edward probably found new work for Master James in Scotland.

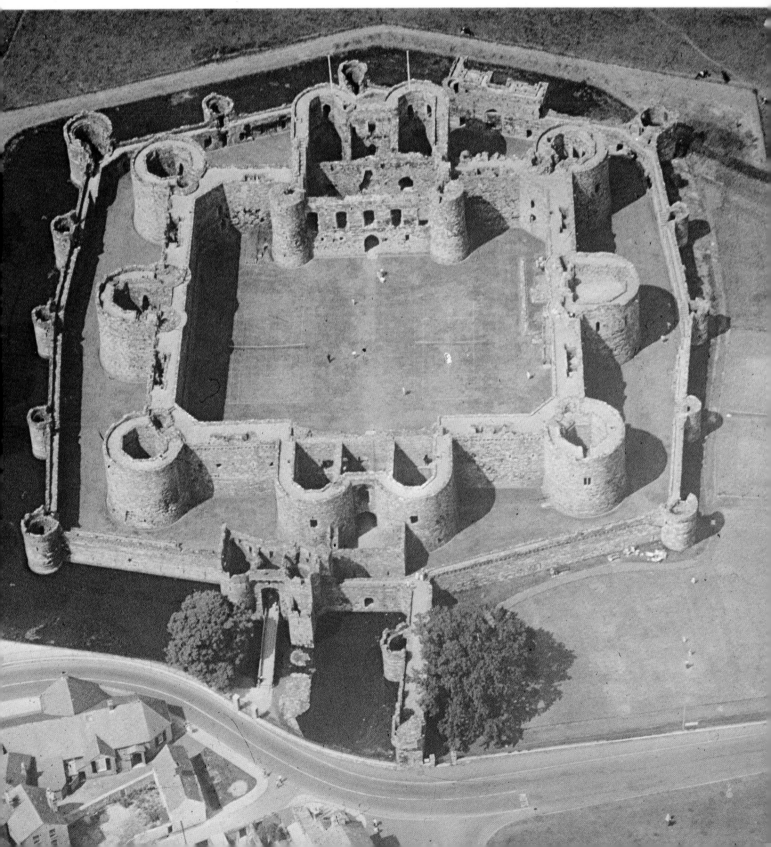

The Birth of the Universities

The progress of learning and demands from pupils in schools caused universities to develop in the twelfth century. Salerno in Italy was Europe's first university, closely followed by Bologna, Paris and Oxford. There seems to be no precise date for Oxford but it developed earlier than Cambridge and both were well-established in the thirteenth century.

At first, there were no university buildings; students lived in rooming-houses and boarding clubs which developed into colleges; they assembled for classes in hired halls, sitting at their master's feet, and, since books were expensive, much of the learning was by discussion. Subjects included grammar, rhetoric, logic, arithmetic, geometry, astronomy (mixed with astrology) and music. At Oxford, some work was done in physics and alchemy, the forerunner of chemistry.

Most of the students were poor, ambitious and unruly. Intense ill-feeling between the townsfolk and students ("town" and "gown") led to riots and, on occasion, to a university taking itself off to another town. Henry III gave royal protection to the universities and great authority to Oxford's Chancellor.

A 13th century carving showing student life in Paris: on the left, students engage in a disputation or learned argument, on the right, they may be attending a lecture and, above, they adopt the casual poses of students in every age.

The university at Paris had close connections with Oxford; students went to and fro freely, took the same degrees and were both governed by a corporation of masters responsible for all university affairs. When Paris students were "dispersed", following trouble with the citizens, Henry III invited them to the English universities. The Hundred Years' War put an end to these close ties and Oxford's reputation drew ahead of that of Paris.

Merton College, Oxford (right), with the oldest quadrangle in the University. The College was founded in 1264 by Walter de Merton, Bishop of Rochester, for secular clergy, i.e. for parish priests, not monks. Its charter (below) became a model for future colleges.

Below right, you can see valuable books chained to the shelves of Merton's 14th century library. By then, Merton was known as "the most distinguished house of learning in England."

The Welsh Struggle for Freedom

Despite claims to overlordship by English kings and attempts at conquest, Wales had kept its independence until Edward I's campaign. Welsh geography and climate had been valuable allies, for, in mountainous, rainy country, invading armies became lost and bogged down. The Welsh were elusive foes. Nimble and lightly-armed, they could move rapidly in any direction to evade an army or to launch a raid on their foes.

Much of the borderland and the southern plain had been conquered by Norman barons, whose Marcher lordships, as they were called, formed a buffer state between England and Wales. But the heart of Wales remained free, and whenever an English king—Stephen or John or Henry III—was weak or preoccupied with his own troubles, the Welsh princes took the chance to pay off old scores, to harry the borderlands and to enlarge their little kingdoms.

Thus, between 1066 and 1282, several Welsh heroes won renown and Welsh independence often seemed secure. And so it was, until there arrived an English king with the resources and tenacity to succeed where his forbears had failed.

Coat of arms of Gruffydd ap Cynan, King of Gwynedd, who led a revolt against the Normans in William Rufus' reign. Henry I invaded Gwynedd but Gruffydd kept his kingdom intact.

Coat of arms of Rhys ap Tewdwr, King of Deheubarth, and recognised as lord of South Wales in the Domesday Book.

A Welsh prince dispensing justice: an illustration from the Laws of Hywel the Good (d. 905), who ruled most of Wales, collected its laws together and was a friend of Edward of Wessex.

The great uprising

Against the ancient kingdoms of Gwynedd, Powys and Deheubarth, William the Conqueror set up Norman earls who pressed into the country. The Welsh resisted fiercely, and Gwynedd regained its independence but, by Stephen's accession, it seemed as if the rest of Wales was virtually conquered.

Then occurred the great uprising. In the south, Rhys ap Gruffydd made himself sole ruler of Deheubarth; known as "the lord Rhys", he held on to his conquests and ruled from a fine castle at Cardigan. In the north, Owain Gwynedd, son of an earlier hero, extended his kingdom almost to Chester.

Llywelyn on his deathbed.

Llywelyn the Great

In King John's reign, there arose ap Llywelyn ap Iorwerth, "the Great", as he came to be called. Grandson of Owain Gwynedd, he became master of Snowdonia and then, having done homage to John, he conquered Powys. John turned against him, and, aided by jealous Welsh princes, forced him to accept humiliating terms.

However, when the Welsh realised they were helping an English conquest, they rallied to Llywelyn who recovered all the lost lands, including South Wales. Llywelyn died in 1240, having done homage to the infant Henry III, in return for confirmation of his conquests.

Here we see a squire who has shown great valour in battle, being knighted on the field. The Norman barons, given more or less a free hand in Wales and the Marches, introduced their own methods and rules of warfare, built castles, disputed the rich valleys with the Welsh princes and formed little colonies to settle and protect the lands they had won. They were often thrust back by the Welsh.

Murderous feuds

Wales was a difficult land to conquer and equally difficult to unite. It had long been divided into a number of small kingdoms and, since Welsh law allowed kingship to be shared between all royal sons, the kingdoms were perpetually torn by murderous feuds.

The success of one prince would arouse such hostile jealousy in his rivals that they would turn for help to the Marcher lords. The greatest of these were the earls of Chester, the Mortimers, the Clares and the Braose family, who made use of Welsh quarrels to increase their hold on the country.

Only occasionally could an outstanding leader, like Owain or Llywelyn the Great persuade the Welsh people to unite against the common enemy.

Bruce at Bannockburn (above): the Scottish victory did not rouse the Welsh—Edward I had done too well.

This little Welsh castle (left) at Dolbadarn could not hold out for long against Edward's offensive.

Empty treaties

In their fight for survival, the Welsh looked not merely to their mountains and occasionally to Ireland, but to their obvious allies in Scotland and France. Thus, in 1168, Owain Gwynedd offered to help the King of France who was at war with Henry II and, in 1212, when John was planning a campaign against Llywelyn the Great, a treaty was made between France and Wales.

A similar treaty of friendship was arranged with the Scots in 1258, against the English. However, when Edward I embarked upon the conquest of Wales, the Scots do not seem to have sent assistance to their allies, and in the English armies that later invaded Scotland, there were many companies of Welsh archers.

The last Welsh rising took place in 1295 but no help came from France or Scotland; the treaties had been little more than an expression of dislike for the English.

Edward Conquers Wales

The rebellion of Llywelyn ap Gruffydd, grandson of Llywelyn the Great, had its origins in Henry III's reign. Llywelyn followed his grandfather's policy of attacking the Marcher lordships and extending his own authority until he could claim to be "Prince of Wales". He played such a prominent part in the barons' war that Prince Edward felt it prudent to acknowledge his gains.

Thus encouraged, Llywelyn refused to pay homage when Edward came to the throne, claiming that the king was sheltering his traitor brother, David. Edward resolved to act. With masterly organisation, he struck at the south and in the centre to crush or win over the lesser princes and then advanced in such strength along the north coast that Llywelyn was forced to surrender. Edward behaved mildly, demanding only homage and the handing back of newly-won territories, but the officials whom he left to pacify and organise the country treated the Welsh so harshly that they soon broke into revolt. This time, there was no mercy. Llywelyn was killed, David died horribly and Wales was brought under English rule.

The warrior king, Edward I, on horseback. When not at war, he was a great patron of tournaments and hunting.

A sudden attack

After the first uprising, Edward allowed Llywelyn to keep Anglesey and his title Prince of Wales. But his brother David made himself the champion of all Welshmen with a grievance and it was he who raised the revolt of 1282.

Without warning, he attacked and captured Hawarden Castle; the Welsh rose to arms and Llywelyn re-entered the fray to organise guerrilla warfare and destroy castles.

The revolt took Edward by surprise and he was furious at what he considered the treachery of Welshmen whom he had pardoned. At speed, he marched into Wales and Llywelyn, determined not to be trapped again in Snowdonia, broke

After Llywelyn the Last was killed in a skirmish, his head was sent to London, paraded through the streets and set high on the Tower of London.

south to join his allies. In a wood, he met some English troops and turning back, he ran full-tilt into a knight who killed him instantly. His death discouraged the Welsh and, although David carried on the struggle, he was eventually trapped and handed over to the English. Dragged by horses to be hanged, his body was cut into quarters and his head set beside his brother's on the Tower of London.

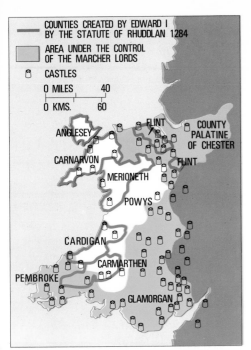

Wales conquered, divided into shires and dominated by the Marcher lords.

A plan for Wales

With Llywelyn "the Last" and his brother David dead, Edward was free to put into operation his plan for Wales. Llywelyn's district was divided into three shires—Anglesey, Caernarvon and Merioneth and the southern part of the principality into Cardigan and Carmarthen.

The four much fought-over districts or cantreds in the north became Flint, part of Cheshire and new Marcher lordships, including Denbigh, where a fine castle and town were built by Henry de Lacy, a baron whom Edward trusted to keep the district in subjection.

English law took the place of Welsh and county courts replaced the judgements of Welsh princes.

To encourage the Welsh to give up raiding and their semi-nomadic way of life, Edward founded a number of towns which he populated with English settlers who were to foster crafts and trade.

The mountainous area of Snowdonia was encircled by a ring of castles—Aberystwyth, Harlech, Conway and Rhuddlan, while the Menai Straits, separating the mainland from Anglesey, were dominated by the fortresses of Beaumaris and Caernarvon.

In general, Welsh law and custom were unaffected by the conquest and there was no feeling of unbearable oppression. However, a local dispute or a court decision could awaken a sense of injustice and Edward had to suppress two more uprisings. Neither became a national rebellion but, while the Welsh remained quiet for a century, their national spirit was by no means crushed.

Caernarvon Castle, from the east, commanding the estuary; from battlements and arrow-slits in angled walls, defenders could direct cross-fire at every yard of ground below the main castle.

Prince of Wales

The size of Caernarvon Castle suggests that Edward intended to make it the government headquarters of Wales.

His son Edward was born there, and this gave rise to the story of the King, having promised the Welsh a prince "that was born in Wales and could speak never a word of English", presenting them his newborn son. True or not, young Edward was formally named Prince of Wales in 1301, from which date the title has always been bestowed on the monarch's eldest son.

The Feudal World

In this book, we have been following the history of Britain during the reigns of eight kings who followed William the Conqueror—his sons, William Rufus and Henry I, his grandson Stephen, Henry II, the Plantagenet, and his sons, Richard I and John, then Henry III and Edward I.

At the beginning, all wealth and power was held by a foreign king and a foreign aristocracy but, by the end, an English king ruled a prosperous land with an expanding population, fine towns and churches, growing trade and rising universities. He ruled but, thanks to Magna Carta, ruled according to law and with the counsel of Parliaments.

In these 220 years, the English became a nation, the Irish and Welsh were partially conquered, and the mixture of peoples in the north became proud to be called Scots. Yet, it was a very different world from ours. Money counted far less, service and duties far more; freedom and independence had little meaning, religious faith and the Church's power entered into every corner of life. This was a feudal world, a time when medieval civilisation reached its height.

Milestones of the period

What are the milestones which mark this period of British history? In Henry I's reign, the loss of the White Ship changed its course, brought civil war, the succession of the Plantagenets and England's involvement in France.

Becket's murder increased the power of the Church, but Richard I's Crusade was less important than his granting of charters to towns.

John's defiance of custom and law caused the barons to set out their rights in Magna Carta and men took them to mean the rights of all Englishmen. Wales came under English rule but Wallace and

Magna Carta, the most famous document in history. Four original copies still survive, two of them in the British Museum.

Bruce defied the English king. Parliament began to take shape, guilds ruled the towns, universities were born and Gothic cathedrals reached upwards to the sky.

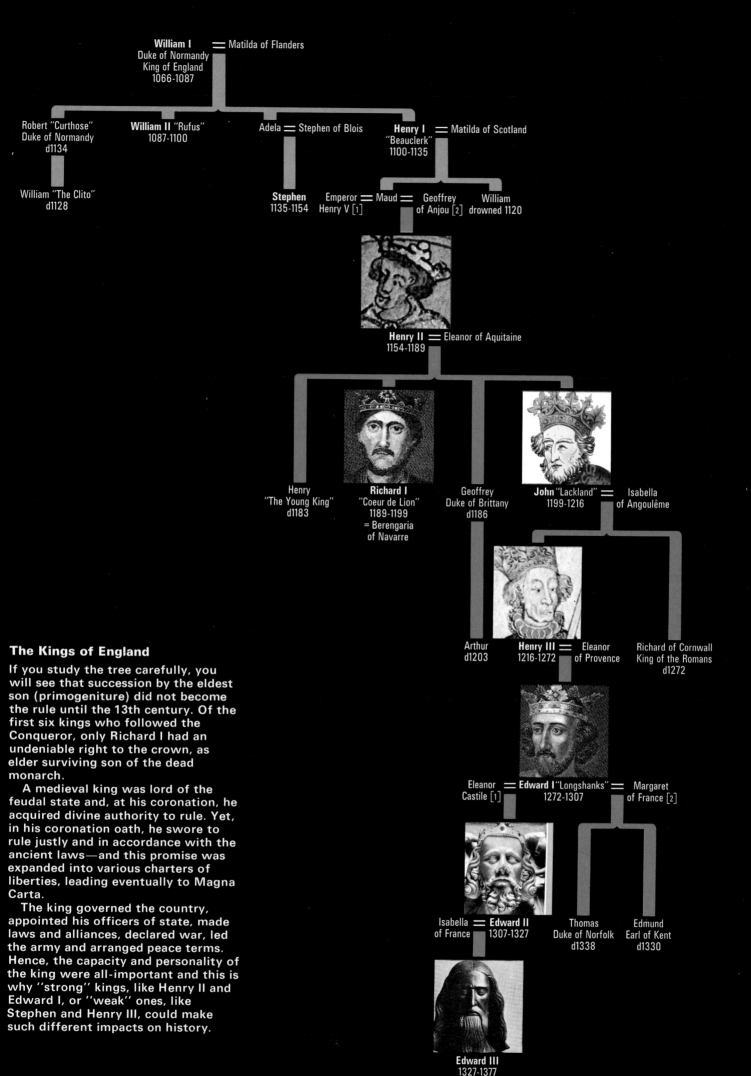

William I
Duke of Normandy
King of England
1066-1087 ═ Matilda of Flanders

Robert "Curthose"
Duke of Normandy
d1134

William II "Rufus"
1087-1100

Adela ═ Stephen of Blois

Henry I
"Beauclerk"
1100-1135 ═ Matilda of Scotland

William "The Clito"
d1128

Stephen
1135-1154

Emperor ═ Maud ═ Geoffrey
Henry V [1]   of Anjou [2]

William
drowned 1120

Henry II ═ Eleanor of Aquitaine
1154-1189

Henry
"The Young King"
d1183

Richard I
"Coeur de Lion"
1189-1199
═ Berengaria
of Navarre

Geoffrey
Duke of Brittany
d1186

John "Lackland" ═ Isabella
1199-1216   of Angoulême

Arthur
d1203

Henry III ═ Eleanor
1216-1272   of Provence

Richard of Cornwall
King of the Romans
d1272

Eleanor ═ **Edward I** "Longshanks" ═ Margaret
Castile [1]   1272-1307   of France [2]

Isabella ═ **Edward II**
of France   1307-1327

Thomas
Duke of Norfolk
d1338

Edmund
Earl of Kent
d1330

Edward III
1327-1377

The Kings of England

If you study the tree carefully, you will see that succession by the eldest son (primogeniture) did not become the rule until the 13th century. Of the first six kings who followed the Conqueror, only Richard I had an undeniable right to the crown, as elder surviving son of the dead monarch.

A medieval king was lord of the feudal state and, at his coronation, he acquired divine authority to rule. Yet, in his coronation oath, he swore to rule justly and in accordance with the ancient laws—and this promise was expanded into various charters of liberties, leading eventually to Magna Carta.

The king governed the country, appointed his officers of state, made laws and alliances, declared war, led the army and arranged peace terms. Hence, the capacity and personality of the king were all-important and this is why "strong" kings, like Henry II and Edward I, or "weak" ones, like Stephen and Henry III, could make such different impacts on history.

85

Time Chart: the main events in world history

British Isles and Ireland

Castles dominated the land, for this was a period when barons fought each other and the king; they also took part in foreign wars. Magna Carta proclaimed their rights and forced kings to rule within the law. The period also saw the rise of Parliament, of towns, universities and guilds; the Scots emerged as a nation and the Irish continued to fight the invader.

1087	Death of William I—revolt by Norman barons.
	William II at war with Robert of Normandy. Anselm, a great archbishop.
	Edgar ruled Scotland as vassal of Wm. II.
1100	Norwegians seized Isle of Man, raided Ireland.
	Henry I m. Matilda of Scotland, defeated Robert of Normandy at Tinchebrai.
	War with France, country well governed—Exchequer system introduced— royal courts and justices. Growth of trade.
1120	Disaster of the White Ship.
	David I introduced Anglo-Norman ways into southern Scotland.
	Matilda, daughter of Henry I, m. Geoffrey Plantagenet.
	Cistercian abbeys built.
1135	Henry I died, Stephen seized throne, civil war between followers of Stephen and Matilda; illegal castle-building and bad government.
	Matilda besieged at Oxford.
	David I of Scotland built Melrose Abbey.
1150	Turlough of Connaught supreme in Ireland.
	Treaty of Wallingford between Stephen and Henry of Anjou.
1154	Henry II became King of England, Lord of Scotland and Wales, with vast possessions in France.
	Becket made Chancellor, order restored, illegal castles razed, jury system in use.
	Becket, Archbishop of Canterbury, quarrelled with Henry, fled abroad.
	Oxford University founded.
1170	Murder of Becket.
	Strongbow captured Dublin, Henry II in Ireland, made Strongbow do homage; civil war in Ireland.
	Barons rebelled unsuccessfully; William the Lion captured. Dover castle and many others built.
1189	Rebellion of Henry's sons; his death at Chinon.
	Richard I granted town charters to raise money for Crusade.
1200	Accession of John *(1199)*. Llywelyn the Great in Wales.
	Arthur of Brittany murdered. French possessions lost.
	England under Papal interdict. John invaded Scotland, excommunicated, submitted to Pope. Barons' revolt—
1215	Magna Carta—civil war—death of John.
	Cambridge University founded.
1216	Accession of Henry III—French driven out. Hubert de Burgh ruled as Justiciar.
	Franciscan friars in England.
	Magna Carta re-issued.
	Glass-making and church-building in England.
	Roger Bacon, scientist, at Oxford.
	Henry III defeated in France. Welsh virtually independent.
	Alexander III, King of Scotland.
	Truce between England and France.
1250	Work began on present Westminster Abbey.
	Civil War in England; Simon de Montfort defeated Henry III at Lewes, called a Parliament and was
1265	killed at Evesham.
	Llywelyn, Prince of Wales, raided the border country.
	Last Norwegian invasion of Scotland defeated.
1272	Edward I, a great ruler, soldier and legislator, invaded Wales, defeated Llywelyn, built castles and founded towns to achieve permanent conquest.
	He awarded Scotland's crown to John Balliol; invaded Scotland, deposed Balliol and declared himself King.
	Scots rebelled but Wallace defeated at Falkirk.
	War with France over Gascony; Edward in dire financial trouble.
	Expulsion of Jews from England.
	The Model Parliament, a representative assembly;
1300	Edward confirmed Charters of Liberty.

Europe

Popes, kings and princes fought incessant wars and organised one Crusade after another. Yet art, learning, building, and merchant cities in Italy and Germany flourished.

Pope Urban II preached Crusade.
The People's Crusade failed.
El Cid fought Moors in Spain.

Cistercian Order founded.
Florence became a republic.
Matilda m. Henry V, Emperor.

Constantinople the most cultured city in Europe.
W. front of Chartres Cathedral built.
Rise of Hohenstaufen family in Germany.
Normans began conquests in S. Italy.
Abelard condemned for heresy.
First tapestries and clocks.
Medical school at Bologna.

Rise of N. German trading cities.
Nicholas Breakspear, Englishman, became Pope.
Paris University founded.
Frederick I (Barbarossa), Emperor, extended German power and prestige.

Rise of Italian city-states, Pisa, Genoa, Florence, Venice.

Louis VII, King of France.

Roger of Salerno writing on surgery. German and French set out on 3rd Crusade; Barbarossa drowned; Richard I captured; war with France.

Venice organised Fourth Crusade and sack of Constantinople.
St Francis founded Franciscan Order.
Innocent III, a great Pope.
Frederick II (Stupor Mundi), a brilliant, arrogant emperor, was bitterly hostile to the Pope; he invaded Italy, conquered Sicily.
Frederick III of Castile defeated Moors and began to unite Spain.
Mongols invaded Poland, Hungary.

Moors in Spain began to build the Alhambra, at Granada. Gothic architecture.

"Saint" Louis IX of France prepared a Crusade.

War between Genoa and Venice.
Long struggle between emperors and popes led to a lack of unity in Germany.

Philip IV made alliance with the Scots.
Venetian galleys traded with England; Italian merchants lent money throughout Europe.

Crusaders retired to Cyprus.

Asia

While the Crusaders fought on in Palestine, hordes of Mongols burst out of central Asia to threaten eastern Europe and to overrun China, without breaking its marvellous civilisation.

A water-driven clock in China.

First Crusade captured Jerusalem.

Crusader states (Outremer) founded.
Knights Hospitallers in Jerusalem.
Sung dynasty in China, fine porcelain, landscape painting; tea widely used.

Ch'ing dynasty founded in China.

Ch'in mastered much of China; Sung court moved to Hangkow.

Second Crusade, disaster in Asia Minor.

Possible use of explosives in China, printing with movable type.

Minamoto family controlled Japan.
Moslem conquests in India.
Saladin defeated Crusaders at Hattin, captured Jerusalem.
Third Crusade; Acre taken, Richard defeated Saladin but unable to re-capture Jerusalem.

Mongol invasion of China by Genghiz Khan.

Islamic rulers built beautiful mosques in Delhi.
Sixth Crusade, Frederick II took Jerusalem, crowned King.
Mongols conquered Russia.

Jerusalem re-taken by Moslems.

Ottoman Turks in Asia Minor.

Baghdad destroyed by Mongols.
Prince Edward on 8th and last Crusade.

Kublai Khan established Yuan (Mongol) dynasty in China with capital at Peking.

Marco Polo at Kublai's court.

Acre, last Crusader possession, captured by the Mamelukes.

Chinese using mariner's compass.

Africa

North Africa was ruled by the Moslem conquerors who successfully resisted Crusader invasions of Egypt. They penetrated far into West Africa, establishing an empire.

Islamic conquest of West Africa by Almoravids: break-up of Ghana empire.

Egypt ruled by Fatimid dynasty, Moslems hostile to the Seljuk Turks but anxious to avenge loss of Jerusalem.
Cairo and Alexandria great trading and industrial cities, making glass, pottery, metalwork, linen, brocades. They controlled the Far East trade by sea and owned a powerful fleet.

Tunis and Tripoli seized by Normans.

Saladin ruling in Cairo.

Trade treaty between Egypt and Venice.

Fifth Crusade in Egypt ended in failure.

Sumanguru, greatest ruler of Soso, a W. African empire.

7th Crusade: Louis IX captured at Cairo.

Sultan of Egypt defeated Mongols.
Louis IX, crusader, died at Tunis.

Mandingo empire centred on Timbuktu.

The Americas

The Maya civilisation declined, but in Mexico and Peru, the Aztec and Inca peoples built colossal stone cities, studied astronomy and mathematics, made fine pottery and textiles.

Chimu peoples created coastal empire in Peru.

3rd Pueblo period: cave-dwellers in New Mexico.
Sinchi Roca, first Inca ruler in Peru.
Huge stone buildings in Cusco.

Maya civilisation in decline.

Toltec invaders established capital in Maya city, Chichen Uza, and introduced war gods and human sacrifice.

Inca tribesmen settled in Cuzco valley; built vast fortresses, using tools of stone. Later, they came to use bronze.

Incas fought wars of expansion.
Aztecs entered Mexico and settled on islands in Lake Texcoco.

Toltecs, in decline, abandoned Chichen Itza.

War between city-states in Mexico.

Aztecs building temples and houses of rubble and mortar, faced with stucco; worked silver and gold, produced fine pottery, textiles and picture writing. Their war-god required innumerable human sacrifices.

Aztecs began to build their capital, Tenochtitlan.

Index

Page numbers given in italics indicate that the item is referred to in a caption only.

Europe

SCOTLAND

IRELAND

WALES

ENGLAND

NORWAY

SWEDEN

DENMARK

FLANDERS

NORMANDY ② ①

③ ⑥

④ ⑤ ⑦

⑧

⑨

⑩

⑪

FRANCE

HOLY ROMAN EMPIRE

AUSTRIA

⑬

⑫

PYRENEES

SPAIN

ITALY

⑭

A glossary of places mentioned in the text

① Bouvines
② Boulogne
③ Caen
④ Falaise
⑤ Rouen
⑥ Mantes
⑦ Gisors
⑧ Paris
⑨ Tours
⑩ Poitiers
⑪ Limoges
⑫ Toulouse
⑬ Vienna
⑭ Rome